Days Gone By

Days Gone By

Jack Peach on Calgary's Past

FIFTH
HOUSE
PUBLISHERS

Cover photograph courtesy Provincial Archives of Alberta, Harry Pollard Collection, P.3971
Cover design by John Luckhurst/GDL

The publisher gratefully acknowledges the support received from The Canada Council,
Communications Canada, and the Saskatchewan Arts Board.

Printed and bound in Canada by Hignell Printing Limited
93 94 95 96 97 / 5 4 3 2 1
In order to remain true to the spirit of those "days gone by,"
imperial rather than metric measurements have been used in this book.

CANADIAN CATALOGUING IN PUBLICATION DATA

Peach, Jack
Days gone by
ISBN 1 895618–26–6

1. Calgary (Alta.) - History. 2. Calgary (Alta.) -
Biography. I. Title.

FC3697.4.P43 1993   971.23'38   C93–098119–7
F1079.5.C35P43 1993

FIFTH HOUSE LTD.
620 Duchess Street
Saskatoon, SK S7K 0R1

About the cover photograph

For years Calgary's main downtown intersection was First Street West and Eighth Avenue.
Controlling the traffic in the 1920s was the responsibility of a uniformed policeman on "point duty."
At first his snow white, gloved hands were enough to halt or wave traffic onward. Eventually, as traffic increased,
he was supplied with a five-foot portable pole, topped by hand-operated red "stop" and green "go" signals.

The officer had to constantly roll the metal signal pole out of the way of streetcars making sharp left and right turns,
so "point duty" became a busy, high-profile job. The always cheerful constable Dan Finlayson (who died in 1926)
preferred that assignment. His popularity was obvious, as each Christmas his intersection post included
a pile of gaily wrapped Christmas gifts from passing motorists, tram drivers, and pedestrians.

Contents

Contents

Contents

Preface

All my life I have been a squirrel—investigating, collecting, and saving "stuff that might be useful sometime."
As a teenager, without knowing exactly why, I collected brochures, clippings, pamphlets, and monographs
of people, places, and events. Parentally nurtured curiosity and an avid interest in the makeup of our surroundings
spurred much of it. The result is an eclectic collection from school years to the present.

Calgary and its surrounding area, people, and achievements are a treasure house. I have developed
a network of sources thanks to survivors who have discovered my voracious appetite for learning what we are made of
in this part of the West. I am grateful that when my father arrived as an immigrant in 1906 he had only enough money
to buy his train fare as far as Calgary; grateful that he and my mother were married here; thankful they brought me forth
into the era of Calgary's growth from fifty thousand to the healthy part of a million people.
In my lifetime, I have seen Calgary evolve from a knot of pioneers to a collection of one-upmanship-worshipping urbanites
with all the selfish and "me first" sins of every one of today's North American cities.
Yet I detect an imperishable core of pioneering, of derring-do, an "It may work so let's try it" attitude
that knits old-timers and newcomers together to keep Calgary an astonishing mix of community-minded,
volunteer-oriented citizens and enterprising individuals unmatched in Canada.

From all of this I am able to winnow and harvest an ongoing, exciting crop of stories—past and contemporary—
that makes Calgary uniquely "my town." This material is the basis for the flow of historical and social comments
from my enthusiastic pen. A very serious illness in 1957–58 destroyed my memory completely, to the degree
that I would get lost in midsentence with no recollection of the immediate present or the past. A long convalescence

started me on the painstaking process of reassembling my memories. That, coupled with voracious reading to catch up,
restored, disciplined, and enlarged my memory. Now I find I am able to recall with proven accuracy
details dating back to when I was only eighteen months old. I firmly believe that one's memory includes
everything one has ever known since birth. The difficult part is developing a retrieval system,
which can only be achieved through determination and perseverance.

I am often asked how I got involved in the field of historical writing. When I was a member of Calgary's CBC radio staff
in 1977, a news editor asked if anyone could recall a Mothers' Day from years past. I volunteered the information,
and the concept blossomed into more than 790 daily radio vignettes. For several years before that I, who had sold my first
piece of writing at the age of twelve, had had more than a score of my historical articles published in national
and international magazines. Those activities led to projects such as this book, which is a carefully selected compendium
of columns dealing with Calgary and area, published over the years in *The Calgary Herald*.
Not having had any formal training as a historian I prefer to be recognized as a storyteller, an honourable
and widely appreciated profession dating back to the 1700s, before the widespread appearance of privately owned books.

Even Calgary, young as it is, has a history.
We should be aware that today will be history in the eyes, memories, and chronicles
of those who will be here long after we have gone.
So here are some memories—for tomorrow!

The Fire That Turned Calgary's Face to Stone

Calgary never has had pretensions of being a London, Rome, or Chicago but nevertheless, like them, it had its own personal conflagration. On Sunday morning, 7 November 1886, a fire started at Ninth Avenue and Centre Street, and before it was extinguished at noon the following day it had levelled a great deal of the heart of the small town. That disaster spurred pioneer businessmen to rebuild the community in a more substantial way and so was born one of Calgary's early industries, sandstone quarrying, along with the sobriquet "the Sandstone City."

Local sandstone quarried by steampowered machinery, then often sawn, chiselled, and cut by hand, was hauled by horse and wagon to local construction sites. Within a few years Calgary acquired quite a new look, thanks in some part to the rash of school buildings—King George, Sunalta, Stanley Jones, King Edward, among others—located well out from the city's core where Central (later James Short), Haultain, and McDougall, which began as the Normal School, were clearly visible on the low skyline.

Our first sandstone skyscraper was the six-storey Grain Exchange Building financed by William Roper Hull in the hope of wresting from Winnipeg the western grain-trading pit centre. It's worth a pause when passing this fine sturdy old-timer to see its massive doors with their jewel-like bevelled glass trim and, above them, a sandstone lintel carved by Robert John Priestly and his son Norman.

Wesley Orr and James Butlin, an ex-mountie whose farm included a large exposed seam of sandstone on the cliff by the Elbow topped by the district of Parkhill, were the first to set up quarries here in 1886. In quick succession quarries were also established on the Spruce Cliff escarpment, on the steep north bank of the Bow opposite Prince's Island, and out near today's site of the Calgary Golf and Country Club.

Most visible to citizens was Bill Oliver's quarry in the coulee up which the south leg of Crowchild Trail currently runs from the Bow Valley past the naval base. Today the Seventeenth Avenue bridge spans the crease where once a narrow earth-filled causeway for a gravelled road and a single streetcar line linked Glengarry and Killarney with the rest of town. Below it could be seen the stonemasons, a steam donkey engine, and the horse teams hefting the huge blocks on the creekbed floor.

It is said that in the 1890s at least half the tradesmen of Calgary were stonemasons working a six-and-a-half-day week, ten hours each day, for a daily wage of $1.50 to $2.00. The sandstone they worked on sold for about $20.00 a cord and the rubble stone left from their shaping could be bought for $6.00 a cord.

At one time the downtown core of Calgary was predominantly sandstone. The intersection of First Street West and Eighth Avenue boasted three corners in native stone: the Alberta Hotel, the Bank of Montreal, and the Alexander Corner, which housed Molson's Bank on its main floor. The building's owner, Sir James Lougheed, built east on the avenue, naming his sandstone structures after his sons, Clarence and Norman. On the northwest corner of Centre Street and Eighth was the old Hudson's Bay Store, a sandstone

Calgary is at the confluence of several streams that have carved their way through huge sandstone deposits. For years, the formation shown in this photograph provided sandstone for residences and business buildings. In 1932 it was penetrated once again during the building of the Glenmore Dam in the Elbow River Valley. Courtesy Glenbow-Alberta Institute/ND–10–79

building renovated some time ago by the Royal Bank. Across from it stood the Hull Block, soon sold to Pat Burns for his offices. It had a heavy blocky entrance, topped by a curved corner and a clock tower, sandstone of course, set well back from the roof's edge.

Even the Boston architects of our public library, the first in Alberta, specified, in 1910, yellow Paskapoo sandstone from local quarries. The skill and artistry of our stonemasons were called upon for building many structures, such as the rugged old courthouse on the site of today's modern building; the Post Office and Customs building at First Street East and Eighth Avenue; the original Knox Presbyterian Church, where the York Hotel stands today; and the Anglican Pro-Cathedral Church of the Redeemer that arose in 1905. Some of the buildings used rugged blocks, others called for smooth, even-faced pieces and many, such as City Hall, emerged with a variety of sandstone treatments.

Sandstone construction also became the badge of many big mansions in Calgary. Beaulieu, the Lougheed home on Thirteenth Avenue SW, Pat Burns's magnificent residence on its half-block grounds facing Central (now Memorial) Park, and Castel Aux Pres, the Mission district mansion of Mr. Justice Charles B. Rouleau, stipendiary magistrate of the Northwest Territories, were a few of the opulent, almost castle-like homes of early wealthy Calgarians. One, never finished because of personal tragedy (the death of the owner's wife), stood derelict for years, steadfastly defying the weather, on the sandy hill at the end of Rideau Road overlooking the Elbow River. Lindsay's Castle it was called, or Lindsay's Folly, an uncompleted monument to a pioneer doctor who chose sandstone saved from the fire that destroyed the original Knox Church as the building material for his dream mansion.

Hotels, hospitals, railway stations, office buildings, warehouses, and residences arose throughout Calgary, built all or in part of the stone found along our city's stream beds. The plentiful supply of native stone was a natural companion for the huge quantities of bricks made in Calgary area plants. Around the city to this day, where bricks form the walls of our mature industrial and commercial buildings, chances are the lintels, quoins, and sills are of sandstone from one of our many quarries whose short, busy lifetime spanned those years of growth in Calgary between 1886 and 1915. In the meantime, today's costs and building techniques are all but rendering obsolete our once well-deserved nickname.

If at First You Don't Succeed ...

One day when things are going so badly you wish you'd stayed in bed, think of Thomas B.H. Cochrane who, with his wife, Lady Adela, arrived here in 1883. He was promptly labelled a remittance man, one of thousands from the British Isles relying upon mailed allowance cheques from "Home." The remittance men were totally unsuited to frontier life but had to spurn, out of choice or persuasion, the gentle and well-heeled life they had known in Britain.

Typically, Thomas Cochrane was from a wealthy background peppered with royalty and near-royalty. Lady Adela, it was said, had been urged to leave England for having incurred the displeasure of Queen Victoria.

The pair's first venture appeared to set a pattern for their Canadian stay of thirteen years. Tom and Adela bought a fifty-four-thousand-acre ranch southwest of High River, then two years later tried out a forty-nine-thousand-acre spread east of Lethbridge. Neither scheme was a success.

The year 1886 found Tom Cochrane embarking on a totally different course. Some two-and-a-half miles west of the present town of Cochrane (named after a different bearer of the name), he supervised the building of a saw mill. He had chosen the location on the north bank of the Bow River near the junction with Horse Creek. The mill was designed to process thirty thousand board feet of lumber daily from logs fetched from stands in the Grand Valley and Dog Pound Creek country to the north and west.

Tom Cochrane impatiently put up with supplies of logs hauled by local teamsters until he could get a railway built. Once a very steep grade between the mill and the open mouth of the Grand Valley had been prepared, the Cochrane Lumber Company's rail line took shape. Steel was laid for about two-and-a-half miles north, and a turnaround was constructed for the lone steam locomotive that was to power the system.

Beyond that point, westward into the timber stand, wooden rails were fashioned and laid for about two miles for the use of horse-drawn log carriers. The idea was great, until Cochrane learned to his dismay that railway ties and that last leg of wooden rails had gobbled most of the timber the line was supposed to carry!

Thomas Cochrane was not much of a businessman but he was very popular with his loggers. He paid them a flat rate whether they worked or not. If a carter's wood hauler derailed somewhere along the wooden track, nobody was particularly keen to bend a few muscles to help him get the vehicle back on the track. So a derailment frequently jammed the line for such a time as to cause the mill to close for want of logs to saw.

Cochrane was a determined man. Upon learning there was coal in the vicinity, he and one of his titled English house guests bought into a small mining operation nearby. Coal miner Cochrane, the rancher and lumberman, reached the same ending! The coal was of mediocre quality and the seam was very erratic. The working, at the mouth of Coal Creek northwest of the lumber mill, was close to the surface but still the venture didn't pay. In 1888 a spur line of the Betsy Track, as the railway was nicknamed, had been built to the mine face but, here too, the payload gave out.

In the meantime Tom and Lady Adela channelled a lot of their energies into creating a town on the Bow River's benchland close

Lady Adela and husband Tom founded the town of Mitford, just west of Cochrane, Alberta. Upon arriving in Canada, near Pincher Creek in southern Alberta, the Cochranes had attempted ranching but were not very successful. They tried, but failed constantly, to become western Canadians. Left to right (back row): *Lady Adela Cochrane; Tom Cochrane.* Front: *Lord Norbury; Mr. Algernon St. Maur, Duke of Somerset; Mrs. Susan Margaret St. Maur, Duchess of Somerset (author of* Impressions of a Tenderfoot, 1890). *Courtesy* Glenbow-Alberta Institute/NA–239–4

to the lumber mill. But the choice was not a wise one because the river edged it on the south and west, a steep bank rimmed it to the north, and on the east side there was a steep rise with only enough room for the CPR's main line.

The slim townsite measured less than three-quarters of a mile in length and only about 196 yards in width. Still, Cochrane built a store and a hotel, as well as his own quite ornate house, and the little settlement, named Mitford in honour of one of Adela's close friends, began to take shape. A church was erected, the first service being held on New Year's Day, 1893.

The closing of the mill didn't help Mitford's growth but neither did it dampen Cochrane's admirable courage. Past failures notwithstanding, he opened a two-span toll bridge over the Bow River, charging five cents for pedestrians and ten cents for each wagon and team. Business was not brisk. Cochrane, with coal still on his mind, helped open a mine at Canmore in 1892. Had he stayed with it, he might well have augmented his finances, which had been sadly depleted by his unfortunate undertakings. Tom Cochrane turned his back on the Canmore coal venture in 1895, leaving just his name behind to identify a slope in what was about to become a very big operation and the foundation of Canmore's economy.

Cochrane was determined to put the Betsy Track back in business. So, in 1891, the dogged pioneer built three brick kilns and used the railway to haul clay from a deposit in the Grand Valley. The bricks turned out by Cochrane were expensive and low grade.

The run of Cochrane luck remained unchanged. He opened a saloon in Mitford but, by that time, the town was beginning its slide into oblivion. Facetiously, one might ask, What does a man do when he has "bombed" at ranching, lumbering, mining, town-building, bridge-building, saloon-keeping, and brick-making—try politics?

Tom Cochrane did just that! In 1896 he opposed Edmonton newspaperman Frank Oliver, an almost perennial politician in the capital city. Cochrane aimed high, a David taking on a Goliath for a seat in the House of Commons. He lost.

One feels that Thomas Cochrane had just about "had the biscuit" as they say. With Lady Adela at his side he turned his back on the West and headed for England. But even there he didn't quite make it to the top. His sister was lady-in-waiting to Princess Beatrice of Battenburg, the governor of the Isle of Wight. She managed to get him appointed to second spot, deputy governor of the island.

So, if you think you have problems, give an admiring thought to Thomas Cochrane, "the squire of Mitford" who kept on trying.

The Roughest Five Days in the West

*B*efore Canadian Pacific Railway trains steamed into our settlement from the east and, a short time later, linked us through the mountains with the Pacific coast, our commerce had travelled north and south between Fort Benton on the Missouri River's navigation system and Fort Edmonton, from which point boats carried frontier freight across the northern wilderness.

Plodding teams of oxen powered strings of freight wagons the year round between Fort Benton and Calgary. But because of less stable ground conditions to the north of us, our settlement became a transfer point for freight and passengers. Horses and mules hauled lighter loads northwards—mainly in Red River carts instead of the ponderous, ox-drawn four-wheeled prairie schooners—through brushland that in many places was too boggy for heavyweight hauling.

It is said that one freighter tried hauling close to three hundred tons in wagons hooked in tandems of three and drawn by oxen. At the completion of a long and most harrowing trip to Edmonton he vowed that, while such trains were possible on the leg south of Calgary, he would never attempt such a heavy northerly haul again.

Even under ideal conditions the trip between the two centres was a major undertaking along the age-old Indian trail. Explorer David Thompson found, and used, part of the route in 1880 when he trekked south from Fort Edmonton and, near today's town of Ponoka, veered to the southwest to arrive at the trading post of Rocky Mountain House.

The two McDougalls, John and David, often travelled that trail and stayed on it until, in the vicinity of Lone Pine (Bowden in modern terms), they made a southwesterly beeline to Morley, site of John's mission and David's trading post. Later Rev. John McDougall and such traders as Sam Livingstone made the entire north-south journey along what was to become the Calgary-Edmonton Trail, then Road, then No. 2 Highway.

The route was not completely surveyed until 1886 when C.A. Biggar and G.P. Roy were assigned the split job of working south and north of Red Deer River Crossing. But even while the trail took the Indian-inspired route that sought the weather protection of coulees and the easiest stream crossings, a scheduled stage line was established between the forts of Calgary and Edmonton.

Though there was only a trickle of settlers, those newcomers were in need of communication with the "outside world" and their pleas of mail service resulted in the formation of Royal Stage Lines, its founders clearly hopeful of landing a mail contract. A. McPherson, a retired buffalo hunter, and J. Coleman were the proprietors and their first trip, with Coleman at the reins of the four-horse team, left Edmonton for Calgary on Tuesday, 24 July 1883.

The stage coach was a very ordinary wagon fitted with seats for its first two intrepid passengers, J. Herbert and Thomas Dunlop. The transcontinental railway had not yet reached Calgary so Coleman's journey had to end some thirty-five miles to the east, where his two fares could catch some sort of eastbound work-train to the closest passenger stop. He delivered Herbert and Dunlop to the railway construction foreman on the following Monday, 30 July!

Almost from the start McPherson and Coleman had competition. In August 1883 Donald Macleod, an ex-Hudson's Bay Company employee in search of a new venture, opened the Edmonton and Calgary Stage. His inaugural run left Jasper House, Edmonton, at nine o'clock on the morning of Monday, 6 August 1883. There were four passenger seats, in pairs facing inwards, and located at the rear of the four-wheeled wagon, beneath a canvas carriage hood. It was like a hutch at the back end of piles of parcel freight. Motive power was a four-horse team and there was no point in being in a hurry, for you were not due in Calgary for five days!

There were many stops along the way: Brazeau's, Telford's, Lucas's Farm, Anderson's, Barnet's, all ranches ready and able to supply lodging and meals along the trail. In those days Ponoka was

From earliest times, although Fort Edmonton was established ahead of Fort Calgary, there has been strong ground communication between the two centres. Today's air buses link the two modern-day cities in less than an hour. That makes it hard to appreciate the convenience of stage coach service, beginning in 1883, which shortened the trip to an incredibly swift five days. We fail to realize what a long walk it was once upon a time! Courtesy Glenbow-Alberta Institute/NA–1905–1

a stop known as Battle River; Olds bore the name of Willow Creek; and there were inviting stops with names such as Bear's Hills and Boggy Plain.

Macleod hauled express at "ten cents a pound" and, with no reduction for delays or round-trip fare, the one-way tariff was $25 that included "100 pounds of baggage per person." So, after a Monday morning departure, weather and stream-crossings permitting, and having cleared the final stopping point of Dickson's, seventeen miles north of Calgary, you would arrive at the Bow-Elbow junction on Friday before the sun went down.

The northbound trip was much the same, with a Monday morning departure from the Hudson's Bay Company store and a Friday evening Edmonton arrival. Thus the teams and drivers had respite from their jolting shuttle service in the comparative comfort of weekends in town.

The key to a successful Calgary-Edmonton stage was the mail contract and, although the rails reached Calgary in August 1883, Edmonton still received its mail over the well-established Winnipeg-Battleford-Edmonton trail. Calgary's mail was transshipped at the Medicine Hat railhead and taken west by wagon via Fort Macleod. Late in 1883 Alberta mail was routed by train to Calgary for distribution.

That was where Calgarian George K. Leeson entered the picture. Already deeply involved in a Leeson-Scott partnership that carried mail by stage between Qu'Appelle and Edmonton via many Saskatchewan points, Leeson changed the name of the carrier that had been abandoned by McPherson and Coleman to Royal Mail Stage Lines. The new service made its first regular southbound run from Edmonton on 12 June 1884, a busy extension to an already active prairie mail network.

By 1885 the Riel Rebellion was causing considerable uneasiness, so along the Calgary-Edmonton stage route, at Red Deer River Crossing, a new hotel was converted into Fort Normandeau. The Hudson's Bay post along the trail at Battle River was armed and equipped as Fort Ostell. The Lucas Farm stage stop also became a fortification thereafter called Fort Ethier.

In 1886 the Northwest Territories government attempted to improve the trail, but it was a half-hearted gesture because the hope of a railway to span the gap was ever-present. Eventually, in 1891, the rails were completed, except that they halted at Strathcona rather than at Edmonton itself. But despite that inconvenience, travellers took the train, forsaking those dogged and tortoise-paced journeys that marked the enterprise of McPherson and Coleman, Macleod, and Leeson and Scott.

A Funeral Was
an All-day Outing

I can't find Augustus Carney. I know that Alfred Carney was buried in Calgary in 1894, but Augustus isn't listed among the late residents of Calgary as having had a recorded funeral.

The search for Augustus confirmed that Calgary's first graveyard was once located near where the Holy Cross Hospital nurses' residence stands today. But as the little settlement at the junction of the two rivers grew, so there developed a need for a burial ground for those not of the Roman Catholic faith. As a result, about fifty acres were designated for this purpose on the western hilltop now occupied by Shaganappi Golf Course. The rocky soil was a problem, though, and another site was chosen and legally acquired in August 1890. This is where Augustus Carney comes into the picture because the new sixty-acre cemetery site was part of the Carney property that extended on both sides of the Elbow and, today, would be divided by the Macleod Trail and Spiller Road. Incidentally, in those days there was no Spiller Road, just the Macleod Trail that skirted the hill on its eastern side.

The agreement with Carney stated that he could continue to occupy the farm buildings and property for a further two years and to harvest whatever crops were planted there. In return he would undertake to maintain a fence around the city's sixty-acre piece and to see that a suitable access gate was in place and serviced.

In 1892 seventy-five bodies were brought over to the new resting place from Shaganappi, even though the new cemetery was considered rather inaccessible. The only Elbow River crossings at the time were at Mission (where a new iron bridge was being built to replace the original wooden spans) and downstream close by the river's junction with the Bow. Early attempts to build a new span providing direct access to the cemetery were unsuccessful, and funeral parties had to continue using the ferry that preceded any Macleod Trail bridge crossing.

The difficulty there was that the ferry of 1893 was merely a rowboat kept on its route by a cable that habitually snapped, leaving the ferryman no choice but to drift downstream until his craft beached itself. Funeral corteges, of necessity, were leisurely undertakings. When one hove in sight the first ferry trip over to the cemetery was reserved for the coffin and the church minister. The second crossing accommodated the pall bearers, the third and subsequent trips transported the mourners, and the total elapsed time for the manoeuvre depended upon the former popularity of the deceased!

Access to this new Union Cemetery was only one problem; vandalism was another. While parks department employees strove to establish greenery in a graveyard that was little more than a desolate sandy hill, intruders were tunnelling about the place to such an extent that the city was forced to buy a most lethal-sounding piece of machinery, a 1895 model Bourchier and Gouin Gopher Machine that one can only hope was as successful as its ponderous name implied.

In 1899 work went ahead on the installation of a water-pumping windmill on the cemetery hilltop to supply nourishment for the newly planted grass, shrubs, and the eighty-eight trees that constituted the initial planting. That was the year the old Carney farm-

In 1890 Calgary bought land for a new Union Cemetery from rancher Augustus Carney. The first seventy-five bodies were brought onto the hill and buried there in 1892, having been disinterred from beyond the western edge of town on Shaganappi Point. By 1908 the cemetery included a mortuary, built on the crest of the hill. Later, a caretaker's house, tool sheds, and a greenhouse were added at the foot of the slope. Courtesy Glenbow-Alberta Institute/NA–3423–5

house was demolished and replaced, down near the cemetery entrance at the corner of the Macleod Trail and Twenty-fifth Avenue, with a six-room caretaker's cottage and a civic greenhouse for the raising of seedlings for city parks.

The next milestone of note occurred in 1904 when construction began on an iron bridge across the Elbow enabling the cemetery to be linked to town by telephone. The year 1908 saw construction of the sandstone mortuary chapel on the hilltop, in which sealed coffins were stored during the winter until the springtime melting of frost permitted burials to take place. Then, in 1912, a four-columned entrance archway was erected next to the cemetery office, superintendent's house, and greenhouse. Extending towards the still bare hillside was a tree nursery—an oasis of young growth that, in time, would beautify the entire area.

One of the landmark happenings in the life of the Union Cemetery was the appointment by the city, in 1913, of William R. Reader, a dedicated horticulturist who devoted the next twenty-nine years of his life to the greening of Calgary. He was responsible for seeing that roads were extended throughout the cemetery and surfaced with cinders, a popular "semi-weatherproofing" of the era, that seven hundred spruce trees were planted on the slopes, and that extensive water piping was laid.

Under Reader's guidance the output of the greenhouses in the northwest corner of the cemetery flourished to the degree that plants grown there were sold to local residents and florists, and flowers were sent to brighten the wards of our hospitals and other institutions in those post Great War years.

In 1923, as a small boy, I remember being led by the hand down the southeast hill through rows and rows of white wooden crosses in the armed forces section of the new Burnsland section of the cemetery, then back past stone angels and crosses and slabs that marked the graves of people we had known as friends or recognized as household names in the young city.

For years city crews were aided by many citizens who undertook maintenance of relatives' and friends' graves. In fact, during the Depression of the 1930s many families did their own grave digging since they could not afford the necessary cemetery charges. As part of our Wolf Cub and Boy Scout public service jobs we weeded and trimmed grass edges on the weekends. And we were part of the guard of honour in 1923 when the Cross of Sacrifice was unveiled in honour of war veterans. I can still hear "O God Our Help in Ages Past" rolling down the hillside and across town as people sang and said solemn things about the servicemen who had joined the silent population of the Union Cemetery. Much later, in the summer of 1954, another memorial to fallen armed forces men and women was unveiled by the lieutenant governor in the Burnsland section of the cemetery.

Another memorial of a totally different kind is part of that hillside. What had been the northern sandy slope is one of our perpetual gems. In 1939, F. Leslie Sara, columnist, naturalist, and conservationist of the garden William Reader created from such a modest and barren beginning, described it this way:

Today the sandhill is a flower-decked glade where frail orchids and lilies of the valley bloom beneath the trees; where a tinkling brook comes down the slope over mossy rocks, drips musically into dark pools and flows out into a marsh where the king-cups riot and the meadow-sweet sends up its heavy scent. And out in the open where the sun beats down on simulated alpine meadows, rare rock plants from a hundred distant highlands hob-nob in cousinly fashion with the transplanted flora of our own Alberta Alps.

Many come to this garden . . . some to seek knowledge among the collected specimens; more in the spirit of pilgrims where they may find peace and refreshment of soul.

It is an inspiration, this lovely garden . . . And in years to come, it will prove a lasting memorial to the man who created such pleasure for others. For no other tribute to his memory will be needed. For in that quiet glade, "If you seek his monument, look around you."

That garden is a brightly coloured and unique corner of the resting place so close, now, to our towering downtown core. It was built by many others, too: citizens who brought their contributions of plants and rocks from the mountains to add to the hillside beauty.

Augustus Carney, wherever you are, I think you'd like the look of your ranchland now.

Those Multipurpose Flour Bags

"We buy our flour in bags here instead of barrels!" Those words of surprise were written in a letter by Isaac Sanford Freeze, a merchant from New Brunswick who, in the summer of 1883, opened a general merchandise store on Atlantic Avenue in the little settlement of Calgary. The flour barrel was on its way out, and that year bagged flour was brought in from Medicine Hat since no mill had yet been established here. It was not until 1896 that Calgary-made Purity flour appeared on the shelves of our pioneer provisioners' stores.

Well before that a Medicine Hat general merchant by the name of Cousins had been using his flour barrel in an unusual manner. One evening he was confronted by roisterous members of the CPR's track-laying crews who had just been paid and were set for a night on the town. Knowing they would either squander their money or be rolled for it, they asked the storekeeper to take care of it for them until they sobered up. Mr. Cousins, having no vault on the premises, and there being no bank in the settlement, devised a cunning way of safeguarding the money. He labelled each man's poke, rolled it, and stuffed it into the barrel of flour to await each owner at the end of the spree.

The abandonment of flour barrels caused the appearance of white cotton flour sacks. The fabric was strong, flawless, and the coloured printing and trade marks on it didn't matter a bit, as families put empty sacks through one laundering after another until the printing almost disappeared. Especially during the Depression, flour sacks were used for underclothing, dish towels, pillow cases, carriers and, in the direst of straits, as makeshift footwear. In those pre-T-shirt days flour sacks were remodelled into sleeveless undershirts. We covered our parrot's cage at night with an unstitched flour sack bearing a gaudy, colour-printed company insignia. The white areas attracted the bird mites, which were easily disposed of the next day.

During thin times of the Depression I trailed after my father while he shot Hungarian partridges, prairie chickens, and rabbits in the fields out by Red Deer Lake. With great compassion, tempered by hunger pangs, I stuffed them into a flour sack incongruously labelled: "Well Worth the Slight Extra Cost."

Many years before there was a subway under the railway tracks on Fourth Street West, the Calgary Milling Company had a plant on Ninth Avenue where Gulf Canada Square stands today. It was another enterprise started by Peter Prince of Eau Claire Lumber and Prince's Island fame. There was a country-style wooden grain elevator at the east end of the complex. A tall concrete structure hugged the avenue, while between it and the tracks, on either side of Fourth Street, other buildings adjoined one another separated only by railway spur lines. At the far west end of the group was a power house topped by a slim metal chimney stack.

In those days a great deal of Calgary-made flour was exported, and while it was still a young company, Calgary Milling had to expand its output by erecting an extension to the mill on the site of the old elevator. The new structure completely overshadowed the others, towering over the skimpy downtown Calgary skyline right through until the late 1940s.

For decades, the Robin Hood Flour Mill on Ninth Avenue West, site of the city's first mill, was Calgary's tallest structure, towering over the city centre. English sign-painter G.L. Taylor, a resident here since 1900, had the job of painting the mill. Years later, when the storage bins were added, his son Ernie Taylor and colleagues painted the sign visible here by transposing the lettering from an 8 1/2 x 11 inch paper pattern to the cluster of huge concrete cylinders. Courtesy Taylor Signs Limited

By that time Robin Hood Mills Limited had bought the plant and replaced the huge painted messages on the sides of the buildings that read: "The Seal of Alberta — The Faultless Flour" and "Economy Brand" and "Made From Selected Hard Wheat." Replacing these signs were the words: "Robin Hood Flour is Different, Well Worth the Slight Extra Cost."

The next expansion by the mill owners in the late 1930s was the addition of a clutch of concrete grain silos at the eastern end of the plant. Onto the expanse of wall was painted the immense Sherwood Forest archer, clad in Lincoln green and looking, I always thought, not unlike the current swashbuckling movie hero, Errol Flynn. Ernie Taylor of the veteran Calgary firm, Taylor Signs, had been assigned the task of painting Calgary Milling Company signs. The firm had first been hired to paint the Calgary Milling Company slogan in 1914, then renew it in 1929. In 1937 it redid the signs for Robin Hood. The expansive sign on the silo wall had to be plotted on paper in the company's shop so that the finished version would appear flat despite the vertical curves of the silo. The more prosaic side of the mill that overlooked the railway tracks bore the super-billboard-sized basic statement: "Robin Hood Porridge Oats."

In addition to this downtown plant, the Western Milling Company in east Calgary, since about 1906, had been producing 350 barrels of flour daily under the exotic brand names of Rising Sun, Gold Seal, Regal, and Empire. Those names obviously were not plucked out of thin air, for the company had generated a lively export business to China, Japan, and Great Britain, and its multi-million dollar operation towered over the traditionally industrial eastern edge of the city. A branch of a west coast company, the Brackman Ker Milling Company, joined the milling fraternity of Calgary at the end of the first decade of this century and was also located in east Calgary, close to the Calgary Brewery.

It was a time of extravagant claims and flamboyant advertising and sales pitches. I had Jim Ballingall, a twenty-eight-year Robin Hood sales employee, recite one such spiel for me: "Robin Hood Flour is guaranteed to give you more satisfaction than any other flour milled in Canada. Your dealer is fully authorized to refund you the full purchase price plus 10 percent if, after two bakings, you are not fully satisfied." That was the chant heard every morning on the fledgeling national radio network in pre–World War II days when the bouncy "Happy Gang" burst onto the airwaves out of Toronto. It was repeated constantly during the Canadian National Exhibition and other big time bake-offs, when Calgary's millers were jockeying for the favoured spot among bakers and house-wives. They produced special flours such as Family, Baker's, Pastry, and bearing such supposedly alluring names as Keynote, Saskania, Allowheat, Tulip, and (Heaven defend the name!) Peach.

Then along came Spillers the Millers, a British firm, to add new zest to the competition. On the evening of 7 September 1927, Spillers "unveiled" the latest jewel in Calgary's industrial crown, a ten-storey flour mill. Its customary mill floors of beautiful polished oak were ideal for dancing and, as I recall, there were three orches-tras and as many buffets on three of the mill's ten storeys before the machinery was started up. Calgary had a population of sixty-six thousand and every adult was invited to the memorable turnout. Before long Spillers's snowy white trucks were visible all over town but, unfortunately, along came the Depression and after a stormy six-year life the plant had to be closed down.

One of Calgary's early flour makers was Alberta Flour Mills, which lasted only a short time. More successful was the Purity Mill, local makers of Maple Leaf Flour products for eighty-six years. Meanwhile Spillers closed its big Bonnybrook plant and the build-ing stood idle until 1946, when it was taken over by Renown Flour. As quickly as 1952 the mill changed hands again, this time operat-ing under the Pillsbury banner. Yet another change occurred in 1976 when Purity, having outgrown its old property, took over the ten-storey mill as the western headquarters of its Maple Leaf operation.

Our export flour markets have shrivelled, though domestic demand has grown with the phenomenal increase in population. The Ninth Avenue mill was closed on 6 June 1969 and demolished in 1973. With only one flour mill left in operation Calgary is no longer a milling centre.

In an effort to determine the extent of our output I found myself groping through a maze of miller measures including barrels and bags, kilos and tonnes, hundredweights and tons, and sacks. Per-haps the disappearance of Mr. Cousin's barrel down Medicine Hat way started something, even a less "dusty" form of banking! The industry that dominated our skyline at the beginning has had a lot of comings and goings, presumably at the whim of the housewife and baker. Right now I'm reminded of the Scottish toast to survi-vors: "Here's to us. Who's like us? Damn few, and they're all dead!"

Aerial Trailblazers

*T*here is an interesting airborne parallel between our part of Canada and the Maritime province of Nova Scotia. On 23 February 1909, J.D. McCurdy, at the controls of the Silver Dart, made the first Canadian and British Empire aeroplane flight at Baddeck, Nova Scotia. On the ground, watching with thrilled pride, was the man responsible for the historic hop, the Canadian inventor of the telephone, Alexander Graham Bell. It is hard to imagine that less than one hundred years ago such a page was written into our nation's history. Prior to that entry in Canadian aviation's story-book, Bell and some colleagues, calling themselves the Aerial Experimental Association, built a man-carrying kite that, in December 1907, had lifted off the waters of Bras d'Or Lake, Nova Scotia, for seven whole minutes! The aeroplane flight a little over a year later lasted for two minutes.

Meanwhile, here in Calgary in 1906 we had our own aerial trailblazers: twelve-year-old Earl Young and his fellow daredevil, Alf Lauder, fifteen. They built a manned kite and managed to get it off the ground towed by an automobile that thumped across the stony prairie of Bowness. Next they tried to urge it off the field with the aid of an engine, but the whole machine was too heavy to fly.

The aviation bug bit a couple of youths by the name of Underwood, near Stettler. In 1907 they built a manned kite that managed to stay aloft, though very close to the ground, for a quarter of an hour, thus bringing considerable notoriety to their hometown of Krugerville. The Underwoods, like the two Calgary lads, had the idea of boosting themselves into the skies with the aid of an engine. A seven-horsepower motor was not enough and, here again, lack of funds and focused support led to the abandonment of a dream.

We had a successful Calgary flying visitor to the Dominion Exhibition in 1908—a powered airship piloted by local aviation pioneer Jack Dallas. It made five successful passenger flights over the fairgrounds before going up in flames during a hydrogen refilling operation between trips.

There was a daring but shy newcomer from Chicago who was too afraid of being laughed at for his aviation schemes to share his name with the public. This fellow, named Simmer, explained his dream to readers of *The Calgary Herald* under the pseudonym of the "Mysterious Aviator" and put his ideas into reality by building an aircraft with Calgarian J. Gordon Mackie, son of a former Calgary mayor. They built the biplane in a barn on Fifth Avenue East and launched its flying career out beyond Shouldice. Powered by a forty-horsepower engine and completed in 1910, this machine made several successful half-hour flights. Prior to World War I it made several barnstorming flights in the West but had to be dismantled because apparently Simmer had borrowed several of its mechanical components from a United States source.

At about this same time Alex M. Jaap entrusted his life to the efficiency of a Gibson multiplane that he took aloft from a pasture a couple of miles north of the city in 1911. The best way to describe the multiplane is to liken it to an open Venetian blind. It was the brainchild of William Wallace Gibson of Victoria, BC, the designer and builder of Canada's first successful aero engine. Gibson had become a prosperous mining and railway building engineer but

Left to right: *Pilot A.J. Smith with rancher Baron Josef Csavossy's own Gypsy Moth CF-ADU and its owner; Curtiss Robin C-EAIG with air engineer George Hoskins; Stinson Detroiter G-CANI, owned by brewer Emil Sick, with pilots Fred McCall and J.E. Palmer. The 1929 photo depicts Calgary's airfield at the time, the Banff Coach Road Airport.* Courtesy Glenbow-Alberta Institute/NA-1258-22

gave up his career to fulfil a burning desire to make a name for himself in aviation. His first aircraft, powered by his own engine, was driven by a pair of counter-rotating propellers in tandem. It met a thorough and premature end on the Pacific coast in a grove of trees. So it was back to the drawing board for Gibson, who came up with the grotesque multiplane powered by the rescued two-stroke, six-cylinder, sixty-horsepower engine.

He brought it to Calgary and, with the help of Ontario-born Jaap, nursed the aircraft through several short, successful hops. On 12 August 1911, Alex Jaap took the multiplane to a height of one hundred feet, then came in for a landing. Too late he saw that the field by Nose Hill was honeycombed with badger holes. The engine wouldn't restart and the machine thumped into swampy ground that reduced it to kindling, for the entire plane was made of silver spruce.

Jaap walked away with a few bruises, but Gibson's wallet was fatally injured and he too walked away. It's a pity because Gibson was an outstanding experimenter and the caper was perfectly timed to coincide with the 1911 sponsorship by *The Calgary Daily Herald* of the city's first airmeet and that year's theme of aviation at the Calgary Exhibition. As part of that focus of attention a French aviator, Didier Mason, was hired to perform stunt flying over the heads of the fairgrounds crowd in a Gnome-powered biplane.

Another gravity-defying hero of those early days was Captain Ernest Hoy, who, though not a Calgarian, helped put our city on the aviation map. On 7 August 1919 he took off from Vancouver in an open cockpit plane bound for Alberta with a tiny cargo of commemorative mail. His ninety-horsepower engine boosted him across the mountains in this very first attempt to span the spine of the continent by air.

He landed at improvised refuelling stops at Vernon, Grand Forks, and Cranbrook, and thirteen hours and nine minutes later rolled to a stop in Lethbridge. Since the trip was jointly sponsored by *The Vancouver Daily World, The Lethbridge Herald,* and *The Calgary Herald,* his flight had to end here in the foothills city. The veteran of Royal Flying Corps combat in World War I and holder of the Distinguished Flying Cross successfully completed his journey on the flats at Bowness. The highest altitude he had attempted was only seven thousand feet as he pursued a weaving course through the mountain passes navigating only by a pocket watch, the CPR Kettle Valley route—when he could see it—and a contour map devised for railway tourists.

A few years later another World War I combat ace, Captain Fred R. McCall, DSO, MC and Bar, DFC, flew a wartime Jenny biplane on a flight aimed at opening airmail service between Fernie, Golden, Banff, and Calgary. The mountain barricade continued to frustrate attempts at a westward mail service, but as early as 1918 experimental airmail service had been attempted between Calgary and Winnipeg. In 1920 pilot A.H. Farrington, with no navigational aids, attempted to establish a regular service, but it was not until 1930 that a Boeing piloted by H. Hollick-Kenyon made the first official eastbound airmail run.

As a small boy living in Glengarry in the 1920s I used to lie on my back on the lawn in the summer sun thrilling to the sight and sound of a flimsy yellow biplane trotting noisily across the sky. It was the forestry plane outbound from the federal hangar at High River, heading for the forest fire country around Rocky Mountain House. I could picture Elmer Fullerton, the intrepid pilot of that Moth—leather helmet and goggles and eagle eyes—whose name was voiced with awe, for he was another aerial hero.

When old-time birdmen get together the famous names still spell adventure: Jock Palmer, who flew with Fred McCall in the heyday of Great Western Airways, based in Bowness; Don MacLaren of Olds, a wartime ace who founded Pacific Airways in 1921; Stan Green, a pioneer bush flyer who became the inspiration for airframe, motor mechanic, and all other aspiring aviation students at SAIT when it was called "the Tech"; Calgary's Nick Carter, the world's first flying cowboy, who founded the Air Cadet League; Frank Ellis, chronicler of our aviation history, builder and flyer of the "West Wind," an experimental plane he and his sidekick Tom Blakely flew with very mixed success at Bowness back in 1913; Hugh Johnson, a mechanic working on Nash cars in Calgary who fulfilled a dream by becoming, in 1926, the second man to solo as a pupil of the Calgary Flying Club. There are so many others, for this always was a flyer's part of Canada.

Calgary was the starting point of the first airmail flight between this city and the provincial capital, a hop accomplished by aviatrix Katherine Stinson in 1916. This city was also the terminus of the world's first high-explosive airlift when Captain Fred McCall piloted a Stinson carrying one hundred quarts of nitro for "shooting" an early Turner Valley oil well in 1929.

Adventure and trailblazing are our western tradition so it seems logical that here, under Canada's bluest skies, pioneer sky-riding has been part of that history, too.

Calgary's Florence Nightingale

When we were small children growing up here in Calgary my mother appeared able to keep track of us even when we were not within her immediate sight. She explained this ability by assuring us: "I have eyes in the back of my head."

Marion Elizabeth Moodie must have had the same miraculous equipment. She was the first woman to graduate in nursing in Alberta. She trained in Calgary's first hospital, beginning her three years and three months of learning on 23 April 1895.

Recalling her initiation into nursing she wrote:

> As the first pupil nurse I . . . was sent to get what sleep I could in a vacant ward upstairs, as I was to commence my probation by taking charge at night while the Matron and Head Nurse, who had been having a very busy time, got a chance to rest.
>
> An hour later I was roused to make room for a new patient [who] proved to be a woman with double pneumonia and miscarriage of a six month's baby, the child being delivered next day but only living an hour. In the next ward was . . . a man with cancer of the tongue.
>
> Across from him was an Irishwoman with synovitis of the knee, who was an inveterate talker and used to make the most of any opportunity she could get to talk to the tongueless man, till he besought us by gestures to pitch her through the window. The only man downstairs requiring attention at night was a bronchitis case, but the Matron used to retire for the night with the warning that ten minutes must not elapse without looking at him in case he should choke.
>
> Then a D.T. case was put upstairs opposite the pneumonia ward and the probationer was not to go out of sight of his door in case he took a notion to come out and jump over the bannister. All spare moments for some nights were spent sitting on the top step of the staircase by the cancer man's door, in sight of the D.T.'s door and sound of the bronchitis man's coughs.

Talk about eyes in the back of your head! Yet those were the expectations of a young girl facing the trials and perils of a frontier nursing career. Marion Moodie was more than equal to it. She graduated, a class of one, in the office of the superintendent of the splendid new twenty-one-bed Calgary General Hospital, an imposing sandstone building on Twelfth Avenue East, in 1898.

The young girl had helped when the hospital was moved from its original site: a two-storey frame house at Seventh Avenue and Ninth Street SW. It had been bought for $100 by a hospital board headed by pioneer stockman William Roper Hull. This is how Marion Moodie had described it: "On the ground floor there was one ward holding four beds, an office, dining room, which, when needed as such, was converted into an operating room, and kitchen. Upstairs there were four small rooms each holding one bed, and over the kitchen two small rooms for the staff and cook."

The front door of the hospital was a conversation piece, for, when the board took over the house as a refuge for the ill and the injured, it was riddled with bullet holes, reminders of the house's more raucous tenants and of visitors to the frontier town.

Upon achieving nurse's status, Marion Moodie was presented with a large silver medal, the only one of its kind, and with it she

set forth to prove her worth as a visiting nurse. Her fees were $25 for two weeks' maternity nursing and $15 for a week of twenty-four-hour daily duty on isolation cases. One of these assignments took Nurse Moodie by freight train to Banff, a twelve-hour journey, to attend a boy of seven who had contracted a severe case of scarlet fever. That in itself was not significant but the diseased child was staying at the Banff Springs Hotel.

Marion Moodie later wrote:

> The C.P.R.'s dread on the part of the manager was that the fact should become known by the other guests. Two and a half weeks were spent in quarantine, a corridor with eight rooms and a balcony being partitioned off for the entire party, consisting of three ladies, child, nurse and ladies' maid, and the case was successfully carried through to a good recovery while the other inmates of the hotel remained in blissful ignorance of our position.

One of the toughest jobs tackled by Moodie was in the Crow's Nest Pass, where coal miners were constantly running afoul of machinery and explosives. During a year-and-a-half on the staff of a hospital in the pass, Marion Moodie mopped floors, carried loaded coal buckets, emptied ashes and, in a doctor's absence, performed the broadest range of medical duties.

It was there that Nurse Moodie acquired the long-lasting nickname of "Sorelle." A young Italian miner was a very amateur coyote hunter. He chased one prowling animal with a stick of dynamite that he threw with a lit fuse. The beast took off, the dynamite didn't, and Cimette, the miner, picked it up, whereupon it exploded, mutilating his hands and temporarily blinding him. Sorelle, as he named Moodie, sat with him, consoled him when only one eye recovered partial sight, encouraged his attacks upon the English language, and helped him towards recovery.

Early railway men in "the Crow" sought Nurse Moodie's help, too. "There was the railway brakeman," she wrote,

> who obligingly holding a chisel for the engineer, received the blow on his lip instead of the tool, and had to run to the hospital to get a stitch put in before the train pulled out. Also, his friend on another train, who, getting his finger crushed at a small station where there was no doctor, trimmed it off with his jackknife, wrapped it in a clean handkerchief wet with carbolic, and was ready for a more correct dressing when the train reached our town 25 miles farther on.

In her more advanced years Marion Moodie quietly helped many Calgary children launch career studies at a bewildering time of their growth. She extended compassionate and understanding help spiritually and financially while requiring the youngsters to follow her stiffly laid out code of behaviour and learning.

During her nursing career Miss Moodie pursued hobbies with the same dedication she applied to her nursing. She was an ardent landscape painter and an outstanding botanist. She originated Calgary's Natural History Society and frequently displayed her collection of over six hundred specimens of Alberta wildflowers, starting with a showing in 1912 at the Natural History Museum that, at one time, occupied part of the library building in Memorial Park. Some of her botanical collections found their way to such prestigious institutions as the Field Museum of Natural History in Chicago and the Smithsonian Institute.

Marion Moodie also was a prolific poetess, collecting and printing many of her works in two volumes dated 1904 and 1934. After twenty-two years of dedicated nursing service in the West, she retraced her steps to become chatelaine for a very wealthy bachelor uncle in Montreal. After his death and until her own passing in 1958, her philanthropic interests were many.

Her writings reflected her fervent love of the West, where she spent arduous but rewarding years far from her Montreal origins. In one Ryerson Press printed collection were these words:

> Glow skies with your golden light,
> Blow softly dear wind from the hill
> For my heart has a longing tonight
> That only the West can fill.

Note: The quotations in this article are taken from Marion Moodie's personal diary "Pioneer Nursing in Alberta."

The Park That Ran on Streetcar Tickets

The route of the Bow River into Calgary is steeped in history. Although it flowed far too swiftly for navigation, the river's down-hill plunge from the mountains carved such a trench through the foothills as to provide, for Indians and explorers, a very accessible and inviting passage into the high peak country.

Names such as Palliser, Rogers, Hector, de Smet, McDougall, Rundle, Sibbald, and Kerr are only a few of those who trod its grasslands and woods as explorers, missionaries, surveyors, and timbermen. In later years the ranchers came and, instead of just passing through, settled on its benchlands and shouldering hills, comforted by the presence of the railway and the river.

There was Senator Cochrane's Ranche, the town of Mitford—problem-plagued dream of Thomas Cochrane—the Bow River Horse Ranche, A.P. Patrick's Mount Royal Ranche, the spreads of Oswald Critchley, Edworthy, Bell-Irving, Kerfoot, Fuller, D.P. McDonald, Copithorne, all members of a long, illustrious list.

At the turn of the century an Englishman, the Honourable William Beresford, bought twenty-five hundred acres of land south of the Bow River some four miles west of the little city of Calgary. He named his property the Bowness Ranche. On its winding run down the valley, the river created a northern bound-ary of almost three miles to his property, so it is likely William had in mind Bowness on meandering Lake Windermere in Westmorland.

Beresford raised cattle, four hundred or so, ranging across the floor of the valley. The home ranch was an eight-bedroom bungalow with a large kitchen and almost baronial dining and living rooms specially designed for entertaining. The house sprawled within a white picket fence on the river's south bank. From the back door a flight of wooden steps led to the water's edge where a narrow bridge spanned the river backwater beyond which was a large wooded island.

The only access to Calgary from this part of the ranch was a two-and-one-half-mile road up through the wooded hillside to the southeast, to meet the Banff Coach Road. In 1906 the Beresfords decided to return to England and put Bowness on the market.

The buyer was William John Tregillus, who lived atop the valley at Rosscarrock (named after his birthplace in Cornwall). He thought it would be a great idea for him and his family to take over the Beresford place. However Tregillus became so increasingly involved with organizing the United Farmers of Alberta and with the establishment of a university in Calgary, that he had no time left to move the family.

In 1909 Tregillus met two newly arrived businessmen from England, Messrs. Hextall and Shackleton, to whom he sold the property. It was a period of a substantial influx of settlers from the British Isles. The plan was to create a close-in attractive suburb for British immigrants of substantial financial standing. The property was advertised in overseas journals but, by that time, World War I was on the immediate horizon.

John Hextall, confirming his faith in the potential of the area, built his own substantial Elizabethan-style mansion near the site of

Dancing at the Bowness Pavilion was a streetcar ticket per dance. For a while the orchestra was Mart Kenney and his Western Five. Dancing took place in the evenings under strings of multicoloured lights. There was an ice cream/candy counter in front of the pavilion. What looks like water in the foreground of the photo, taken in 1921, is actually extremely fine gravel. Courtesy Glenbow-Alberta Institute/NA–2885–2

the Beresford place. He subdivided the ranch into building lots, with the exception of a clubhouse matching the splendour of his own house, and an eighteen-hole golf course. The Hextall house later became the Woods Christian Home for orphans and abandoned children.

Shackleton was next to sell. Hextall became sole owner, built a power plant to help make the subdivision self-sustaining, and, around 1907, began negotiations with the city of Calgary to provide streetcar service for his residential community. To the east across the Bow River were Hextall's neighbours, James and Mary Shouldice, who had come to the Bow Valley in 1901. James was a large landholder, additionally operating three sections of land on the Blackfoot Reserve south of Cluny.

He and his neighbour A.S. McKay donated one-hundred-acre Shouldice Park to Calgary and deeded one hundred acres to Mount Royal College. Another much-appreciated gesture was that of financing the bridge over the Bow River to link his property with that of John Hextall, next to him on the west.

My parents, newly wed in Calgary, spent many festive weekends in the valley with the Hextall and Shouldice families. Before the bridge was built, the group of young people found it a challenge to cross the Bow in a rowboat or, in winter, on the ice in order to continue partying the following day in either of the very large ranch houses.

The valley itself was the site of our earliest airport, for Fred McCall and Jock Palmer, wartime air aces in search of adventure and fortune, established their charter and sightseeing flying business there. In fact the Fred McCall family spent many summers in a cottage on Bowness Island in the woods to the west of the old dance pavilion after Hextall had donated the park to the city.

R.C. Thomas, an immigrant Welshman, built a thriving business out in the valley across the river from Bowness Park. His Alberta Ice Company was a city-wide supplier. It was quite a sight, in my young days, to visit, on a clear winter's day, the solidly frozen ponds west of Keith (now Robertson) Siding and the tuberculosis sanatorium and watch horses and men with big saws cutting huge blue blocks of ice for Calgary commercial and domestic customers.

As the passenger trains thundered up the hill from Calgary there was plenty to see before too many miles had passed. There was Lowry's gardens, where stooped-shouldered farm workers nurtured much of Calgary's fresh foodstuffs. Next came the whistle stop of Critchley, and the station at Brickburn Town, where the E.H. Crandell and Tregillus kilns made many thousands of bricks that helped create new skylines in scores of towns and cities across the Prairies. The Twin Bridges across the Bow took the train along the north shore opposite Bowness. Then came the gallop up the benchland through Keith, past its sprawling white and red TB pavilions and beyond the ice plant. In those days, before there was such a thing as Bearspaw Dam, you had soon left the city and its straggling outskirts behind as the Bow River flowed swiftly eastward. Your westbound pathway, in the steps of those who had pioneered the route, aimed for The Gap, that unchanging aperture in the east wall of the Rockies.

To Market, to Market

When Mother didn't want to make the long trek into town by streetcar to personally select the week's groceries, she would order them by phone, for John Irwin, the Hudson's Bay Company, and Sunalta Grocery offered free home delivery. One small place that existed somewhere in the west end had a telephone number very close to ours. Careless diallers would call us, and my father, impishly, would put my "uncle" Robin on the line to solemnly take the order. He would discuss name brands and prices with great authenticity, and perhaps there's still someone out there who wonders why the store never did deliver the order. My parents considered the evening calls impositions, and when someone called W4506 by mistake, the order was taken without ever revealing the dialler's error.

In those days there were two dominant food shopping places, the Market and the Market. Somehow housewives could distinguish between the two but I never could. Would we take the Killarney streetcar, identified by a yellow arrow, to the Market? Or would we go to town, then transfer to the Riverside car, marked by a red and white cross, for the longer journey to the Market? "Wait and see" was the standard reply, so I did.

The Market in the centre of town was behind the Clarence Block that somehow in those days seemed to extend right through from Eighth to Seventh avenues. If you entered from Eighth you would be in Miss Snell's dry goods store, where your mother always maddeningly stopped and dallied over Butterick dress patterns. Your only fun was to watch the shiny metal change boxes chittering along the speeding wires, up near the ceiling, that connected the main floor clerks with the cashier on the mezzanine balcony at the rear of the store.

That boring episode over with, you went back through Miss Snell's, out across the lane and, through a pair of swinging doors, into the whitewashed market with its wet concrete floors and nose-twitching array of drooly aromas. This was the Market where vegetable, meat, and dairy vendors had their stalls shoulder to shoulder along aisles that reached from back to front of the building.

Fresh oranges, pungent onions and cabbages, perfumed berries, cantaloup, and the earthy smell of mushrooms mingled with the special smell of freshly killed poultry that hung naked and head down from ceiling hooks alongside halves of beef and lamb and pork from which would be cut the roasts and chops of your choice. "Bones for the dog? Certainly, madam," and a free extra would land in the waxy brown paper beside the scales. "Liver? Here, I'll just add a couple of fresh kidneys," and into the paper they would go.

The vegetable and fruit merchants usually were Chinese, and behind their banks of produce would be lily bulbs. Regular customers would find in their bundles, not long before Easter, a bulb or two. Miraculously those bulbs, carefully split with a paring knife and placed in a bowl among clean stones, would produce a small bouquet of white lilies by Easter Sunday.

The other Market was a much more imposing place. It had emerged from the first public market the town had ever known, an open-air space on Drinkwater (Second Street East) to which farmers had flocked with their meat, vegetables, milk, eggs, and butter in 1885. Soon they were joined by other pedlars, and by 1887

Calgary housewives were clamouring for more sanitary conditions for a public market.

The city's next step was to authorize a weekly open-air sale on a closed-off portion of Atlantic and Osler, that would be at Ninth Avenue and First Street East. A wrangle over hours of operation, location, and sanitation continued for several years until, in 1910, a newly formed consumers' league managed to have the market established indoors in the old Sleepy Hollow school building on Eighth Avenue East, where not only were sanitation conditions

The Calgary Public Market was located on Second Avenue East at the southern end of the Langevin Bridge. Plans were made to transport produce from vegetable and fruit growers in such towns as Carbon, Chestermere, and Strathmore, by interurban trains, but the idea never developed beyond the planning stages. For years, before the market was demolished in 1978 to make room for arterial road traffic, Hook Signs Limited occupied the cavernous building and put the expansive floors to good use as a firm base for billboard painting and assembling. Courtesy Glenbow-Alberta Institute/NA–644–5

enforceable but the customers were treated to weights and measures, too!

In 1913 *The Calgary Daily Herald* reported that " . . . after five hundred Calgary housewives attended a meeting and heckled the aldermanic candidates for four hours, the city fathers decided that a market was necessary."

Mrs. Annie Gale, a Worcestershire woman of great determination and leadership, was instrumental in the move to establish a permanent city market. She saw the endeavour achieve reality in 1914 when a piece of riverbank land at Second Avenue and Third Street East was designated as a market. It was a large brick structure more than half a block deep, tall, spacious—a central place for housewife shoppers to congregate the year round for family food supplies.

I can remember going there in the family car as well as by streetcar. It was a long way from Glengarry but the heavenly aromas were there and the wonderment of sight and sound: rows of meat carcasses, the cries of the vendors, the clatter of the supply carts and trolleys in the cavernous building. It became one of those rendezvous points where one looked for the same farmer's family week after week, and it was a central, precious link between those who produced the food out and around the growing town, and the city "slickers" who came to gawk and assess and to buy. The city Board of Health ensured the high quality of produce sold there, the licensing of vendors, and equal marketing opportunities for producers large and small.

Transportation promoters instantly saw in the permanent market centre an opportunity for new business. For at least two years they had been eyeing the struggles of the city to establish a permanent market place, knowing that when one was finally deemed a success it would be a logical terminus for the foodstuffs hauled in regularly from the surrounding countryside.

They began making plans well before the market site was decided upon. One interested firm was the Alberta Interurban Railway Company. This company had emerged as a rather more practical successor to the proposed Alberta Electric Railway Company, which had grandiose plans of covering southern Alberta. The A.I.R. planned to use the trackage of Calgary's street railway system to bring its produce- and passenger-carrying trains right into town. The Calgary Municipal Railway flatly refused to entertain that idea but not before the upstart firm had voiced its plan to run its trackage across the Bow at the Langevin crossing and along to the proposed market site on the south bank of the Bow River. Decades later the Canadian Pacific Railway was to meet with the same opposition insofar as the riverbank right-of-way idea was concerned.

The Alberta Interurban had hired a traction expert from Britain, C.S. Drummond, and had five crews working on a roadbed between Carbon and Calgary. In the meantime the Alberta Metropolitan Railway Company was stirring up interest in the idea of hauling perishable dairy, meat, and vegetable cargoes into the future central market from the Shepard area.

The Chestermere Calgary Suburban Railway Company, another electric line, was promising fast service of market produce from the "Swellest Residential Suburb of Calgary," and it would bring passengers in from the country too, hopefully beginning the city's first commuter service. The Chestermere outfit raised over $100,000 from rural residents along its route but before long it was tasting the bitterness of failure at the hands of the people it chose to serve. The company imported thousands of hardwood ties and stockpiled them near the Cushing Bridge in readiness for the tracklayers. But within months most of the ties had been stolen by the horse and wagon set that used that road in and out of town from the east. Along with all the other transportation dreamers, the company faded into the land of "if only . . . "

The influence of Annie Gale was by no means lost once the new market was established. She was still heard, and her influence still felt, during her work on such things as the Fair Price Inquiry Committee at city hall. She went on to became the first woman to hold aldermanic office in the British Commonwealth, earned renown as a consumers' league worker, helped organize the Vacant Lots Garden Club (an implacable foe of those who tried to keep food prices at inflated levels), and eventually completed six terms on the aldermanic board of Calgary. She kept an eagle eye and a sharp tongue at work to ensure the high standards of the market were maintained, bowing to no pressure group, for, as she said, " . . . if I had to be endorsed by a political organization to get elected I would go down to defeat."

In due course shopping habits changed and the Calgary Public Market we, as children, had known as one of "the Market" places, lost its customers. The building became a storehouse and headquarters of one of our leading billboard and sign companies. Then, like so many other pioneer structures of substance, it vanished under the sledgehammer of progress. But it had done its job well.

The Canvas City of Sarcee Camp

At one time during World War I there were ten thousand men under canvas in Sarcee Camp on the tableland edging the north shore of the Elbow River west of Thirty-seventh Street. In those days, when the city was small, it was quite a common sight to see troops marching, albeit in not very well disciplined order a lot of the way, the eight miles from camp to the city's centre. Happily for the volunteer troops most of the marches ended at the Twenty-ninth Street loop of the Killarney streetcar line on Seventeenth Avenue West.

My sister and I used to listen for the approaching column of uniformed men. On a hot summer evening they would appear from the southwest and head for the streetcar line by way of our back lane. Mary and I would lug small pails of cold water and a long-handled dipper out to the back gate where some of the dry-as-dust soldiers would break ranks to quickly drain the buckets. "Drinking the soldiers" we called it, a privileged and jealously guarded task because the men in khaki were so appreciative.

On occasion our mother would take us out to the camp, for our parents knew many of the Calgarians in their new uniforms. I, being blessed with an unusually long and quite accurate memory, recall rows of bell tents—so seldom seen nowadays—the spaces between them bridged by slatted board duckwalks; the sound of rhythmically tramping boots and the clear calls of bugles; and the feeling of excitement we were too young to understand in that khaki-clad "town."

One of the parts we weren't taken to was Sarcee City, a make-shift community largely devoted to soldier entertainment. We were shielded from the iniquities that ranged along a prairie trail beyond the north edge of the camp. Wooden buildings stood cheek by jowl housing such emporiums as the Gaiety Theatre and Lunchroom, Expert Military Tailors, D.E. Black's Jewellery, the Club Cafe, Sarcee Shooting Gallery, Pastime Billiard Parlor, Royal Theatre, Turner's Billiard Parlor, and the BB Shooting Gallery. Those businesses did a roaring trade throughout the war years, and the traffic along the storefronts helped imprint in the prairie soil the roadway we know today as Glenmore Trail.

One of the sights we were always shown as children, while it existed, was the camp mascot. It was a live bear cub that, with a collar and chain to restrain it, dwelt on and around an old tree stump embedded at the side of the main thoroughfare into the camp. Obviously spoiled rotten by constant attention and pampering, this creature, little and cute to begin with, soon grew in stature, its physical dimensions enlarging in direct proportion to its temper.

I presume that was the case because the last time I saw the bear it still looked so loving and real that I burst into small boy tears. That was because the bear, now a triumph of the taxidermist's art, stood stuffed and glass-eyed in a realistic post-mortem pose at the foot of the dark wooden staircase rising from one side of the lobby of the old Ogden Hotel, which had been converted into our first wartime military hospital, forerunner to the various Colonel Belcher hospitals that succeeded it.

Part of the longevity of my memory is predicated upon my

Sarcee Military Camp was located beyond the southwest corner of Calgary. At the height of its service, during World War I, the "canvas city" accommodated as many as ten thousand troops-in-training. A tiny village sprang up near the edge of the camp, connected to Calgary by a temporary streetcar line carrying people and supplies. The guns of the 20th Battalion are visible in the right foreground, and in the distance is Bull Head Ridge on the Sarcee Indian Reserve. Courtesy Glenbow-Alberta Institute/NA–989–1

recollections of the Sarcee visit by the Duke of Connaught as governor general of Canada. The golden glint of band instruments, the thunder of drums, the rumble of marching feet on the prairie, and the shouts of command out there in the hot July sun are among my earliest memories. Clutching my mother's hand I stood there watching what, to me, was an enormous sight. My Sarcee recollections are all fine weather ones, for the camp during World War I was a summertime establishment. In winter the troops were billeted, exercised, and drilled on the Victoria Park fairgrounds we know today as Exhibition Park.

As the war years dragged on the newly available streetcar ride to Sarcee Camp was an eagerly awaited treat. The Calgary Municipal Railway, already servicing Glengarry and Killarney with a line along Seventeenth Avenue that looped just short of Twenty-ninth Street West, put in a switch at the end of our road. Fascinated, we squatted on the wooden sidewalk watching as tracks were laid along Twenty-eighth Street past our house and out of sight to the south. When it came time for us to board a streetcar for the trip by rail out there to the southwest corner of the world, it was an occasion for great excitement.

The streetcar lurched and bucked along its temporary track across the empty prairie, ending its journey at a loop on the hilltop above the camp. You could pinpoint the terminus today somewhere close to the corner of Glenmore Trail and Thirty-seventh Street, where the World War II tank sits "enshrined."

In time the city extended the streetcar line down into the camp in order to facilitate the delivery and pickup of freight, for the Sarcee line was a money-making carrier of both cargo and passengers right from its beginning in May 1916 until the end of its useful life in early 1919.

After a while the marching columns were replaced by soldiers jamming each streetcar and trailer to the doors. The military men were bound for fun in town, although a few months before the car service began, one occasion turned into anything but fun when it got completely out of hand.

On the evening of 16 February 1916, a group of about five hundred men, mostly soldiers, erupted in anger over a rumour that a local restaurateur had fired a returned soldier from his kitchen staff, replacing him with an Austrian. The soldiers wrecked the White Lunch at 128 Eighth Avenue and, while the momentum of the vandalism was running at full speed, demolished a dance hall above the restaurant even though it was owned by a Scotsman.

Order was restored late that night but the following evening soldiers from Sarcee Camp, in company with hundreds of civilians sharing an ugly racist mood, descended upon the Riverside Hotel that used to stand on the northeast corner of the intersection at the north end of the Langevin Bridge. Because it was owned by a European whose homeland was at war with the Empire the hotel was sacked by a mob of some fifteen hundred.

One outcome was the arrest and detention by the mounted police of half a dozen rioting soldiers. For a while their angry companions threatened to raid the old court house on Fourth Street West to release their buddies. Some shots were fired and one soldier was wounded but eventually calm and reason were restored. Army and city police patrols toured the streets for some weeks thereafter until the hate campaign subsided, thanks in large part to the peacemaking persuasion of Mayor Michael Costello.

Historian Leishman McNeill used to recount an episode from those turbulent days when Jimmy Hunter, superintendent of the Lougheed Building, with admirable presence of mind, hastily plunged an outdoor electric sign into darkness and had it carted off before soldiers could spot Cronn's Rathskeller in the building's basement. It, too, was German owned and a ripe target for the rioters. Hunter locked the doors and doused the lights, thereby saving the popular night spot from the mob's wrath.

Attention-getting activities of the soldiers we, as children, saw were those of pride not anger. Two miles north of Sarcee Camp is a rather majestic hillside bordering the western extension of Richmond Road. This big hill is the prehistoric slope of the Elbow River's north bank and is laden with boulders under its prairie grass covering.

Soldiers from the camp toiled for many hours in their spare time to spell out their regimental numbers and, having fashioned them into hillside numerals of great size, whitewashed the stones. From miles away one could see these proclamations that "151," "51," "131," and "137" were among the Canadian Expeditionary Forces battalions camped there in the snow-white bell tents off to the south near the Elbow's edge.

These huge letters lasted for several decades, long past the years when the army had originally camped closer to town in what was known as Reservoir Park, near today's Crowchild and Thirty-second Avenue SW; long after the shame of the race riots, the Ogden army hospital, the mascot bear cub; and very long after the last shot had been fired in Flanders.

But for a long time Calgarians knew our city as a garrison town in those days when so many of her young men were locked in battle overseas and more were preparing to join them.

"All Abooard!" the Monorail

Many years ago in *My Wonder Book of Railways* there was an illustration of a monorail train lumbering along on its run between Listowel and Ballybunion, near the mouth of the river Shannon in western Eire. Another photo showed a "sidesaddle" type of monorail train travelling around a curve above water traffic in the German city of Cologne. Those scenes, which I studied so intently all those years ago, have stuck in my mind to such an extent that I viewed the pitch for a monorail in Calgary, in the 1980s, quite nonchalantly.

It has baffled me for some time why our town did not opt for a monorail as our "son of streetcar" project. After all, that form of elevated transportation, clear of our weird ground-level weather, coupled with the success of North American monorails in the aerobus town of Mont Ste. Anne, Québec, and the cities of Seattle and San Diego, seems so logical.

Besides, Calgary has already had a monorail, one that operated with success, except perhaps that it was too far ahead of its time. It was born, lived briefly, and died unappreciated. Even though it was never more than a freight carrier in 1911, the idea of a monorail may still be too innovative for our municipal kind of thinking.

On 22 October 1912, the Alberta Mono-rail Company Limited was incorporated by a local rancher, Walter Moss, who had anything but myopic vision for transportation in this part of the West.

The capitalization of the company was $500,000, and the system Moss proposed was to span the distance between Calgary and Regina with a single-track right-of-way serviced by high-speed vehicles unencumbered by terrain, weather, and local traffic.

In on the venture with Moss were such local worthies as lawyers R.B. Bennett and W.H. McLaws—the former becoming prime minister of Canada—and Clifford B. Reilly, who became a senator of the University of Calgary as well as being a member of the bar in Québec, Alberta, and Saskatchewan.

In order to make a sales pitch to Calgarians the group arranged for erection of a short section of raised track at the Calgary Industrial Exhibition of 1911 so that people might ride their train. They had their multi-ton locomotive hauled to what then was Victoria Park where it and another relatively new creation, the aeroplane, were featured as the exhibition's 1911 "High Class Attractions."

Alberta's minister of the interior, the Honourable Frank Oliver, opened the fair at two o'clock on the cloudy afternoon of Saturday, 1 July, in company with Mayor John W. Mitchell and president of the Calgary Industrial Association, Sheriff I.S.G. Van Wart. Thousands of Calgarians and city visitors attended the opening ceremonies and a record-breaking throng of 23,819 people funnelled through the turnstiles that opening day.

Hundreds of fairgoers were brave enough to try a free ride on the monorail. Cars for it had been manufactured by the Union Iron Works in the city, and although they were designed for freight rather than passenger hauling, it was reported that the adventurers took it all in good humour. The monorail, spectacular though it was, rated only a single line in local news stories that day.

One of the train's charter riders was Beatrice, daughter of Walter Moss, who remembered taking her turn on her father's

On 12 October 1912, the Alberta Monorail Company was incorporated by Walter Moss. The monorail run is visible at the bottom of the photo, parallel to the eastern edge of the Bow River, south of today's Glenmore Trail. The monorail never did carry passengers, except when a section of it was on display at the Calgary Exhibition and Stampede. It did, however, have a short, busy life as a road materials transporter. Courtesy Glenbow-Alberta Institute/NA–2888–1

train. As Tom Moore, historian and columnist for *The Albertan* newspaper, commented after a conversation with her, " . . . the one-track railroad was no dream or just a model, but was a full-scale operating unit that had only one fault—it was too far ahead of its time."

The track at the exhibition grounds was just a sample section of the real route. It was a single thirty-pound rail such as those then in use by more conventional railways, except that it was raised above the ground about five feet on timber trestlelike supports. The locomotive looked not unlike a modern double-ended diesel, only much smaller. According to a 1913 newspaper article, it weighed ten tons and was powered by a pair of sixty-horsepower motor truck gasoline engines, one overhanging each side of the rail, that could be used together or singly depending upon the grade and load.

The train could travel at seventeen miles per hour, although its normal cruising speed was eight according to Ogden old-timer Ernest Russell. The company planned to start a passenger service but first the monorail train was put to work hauling gravel from a river edge deposit at Maharg, a district south of Eighty-second Avenue and west of Twenty-fourth Street SE, to a point near the Canadian National Railway Bridge over the Bow by the old Imperial Oil refinery site. Some old-timers claim that the monorail spanned the Bow and terminated at the Burns feedlot on the west bank of the river south of today's Glenmore Trail East. In any event the monorail track ran along the eastern bank of the Bow for quite a distance and the company hoped it would be extended to link the Maharg gravel pit with downtown Calgary to take advantage of the building boom. There was brave talk of it hauling wheat, passengers, coal, and farm commodities once it had a definite rural route with a beginning and end. Thirty-car freight trains were dreamed of, and those who tried the sample ride at the exhibition were enthusiastic at the potential of this rather revolutionary railway system.

The company, recalled Ernest Russell, commissioned designs for passenger cars, each capable of carrying up to thirty people, to be built here in town along with ten-ton capacity gravel cars with hopper bottoms for fast unloading at city depots. One advantage of the saddle-type vehicles was that the greater the load, the less chance there was of derailment while the gearing of the power car, as the locomotive was called, enabled the train to tackle successfully quite noticeable grades.

Unfortunately years of river flooding have erased the route of the old monorail line. I have discovered remnants of milled wood that might have been part of the single rail roadbed west of the new suburb of Riverbend, for I have learned that the line crossed what then was called Shaughnessy Park, down below the gun club in the vicinity of Eighty-second Avenue and Fifteenth Street SE. It followed the river to a point north of the present-day Graves Bridge.

Its backers predicted that this system, new to the West, would revolutionize travel. Its roadbed was much cheaper than the conventional two-rail right-of-way, and it was not a potential victim of weather abnormalities. It could be suspended, if required, above surface traffic and speed with a disregard for variations in terrain across open miles of prairie that otherwise would be impassable because of winter weather or springtime flooding.

Despite the popularity of the "sample rides" at the 1911 exhibition, the idea was too modern. For a brief time the line hauled gravel, not people. But after all, in those days Calgary's population was only in the fifty-thousand bracket, spread over a wide area and not sure of its future growth pattern.

Investors Captain C. Amphlett, George S. Robinson, and the firm of Stirling and Riley have all disappeared from the scene, along with the trio of farsighted lawyers, as well as Walter Moss— who sparkplugged the undertaking—and even daughter Beatrice Moss—who was better known as a music teacher and Pro-Cathedral of the Redeemer accompanist than as one of the riders of her father's train.

Now we are back to two surface rails with problems of traffic congestion, collision, land acquisition, and acrimonious community associations. It makes me wonder if anyone else looked excitedly at those *My Wonder Book of Railways* pictures. Maybe one day in the future we will look up, too, as monorail trains whiz by overhead.

When Polio Came—We Left!

*I*n a bulletin issued by Hillhurst United Church in the autumn of 1935 was this entry, " . . . the customary Church Supper on Monday, September 16th was not held due to an outbreak of infantile paralysis."

That was by no means the first time such an announcement had been necessary but my encounter with it brought back schoolday reminiscences of this time of year some sixty-odd years ago. When joyful sun-drenched summer holidays at Sylvan Lake or on the farm east of Olds were over it was time to come face-to-face with another school year. Whether we admitted it or not, all of us were pretty excited by the prospect of a new challenge, new teachers, new schoolmates, and renewed friendships.

School opened on the heels of Labour Day, and I recall a special feeling we had about being members of the first classes held in the newly opened Western Canada High School. Although that was five years before the "Hillhurst church announcement polio," as we colloquially called it, had become an annual part of life in the fall of the year. Suddenly, devoid of the drama of its opening, each school was closed before September was little more than half-over. Infantile paralysis or poliomyelitis stalked this part of the land again.

We students were delighted: the leaves were golden, the days were winy with that delicious smell of frost, and here we were, with a reprieve. We were immortal, of course, for we knew full well polio would strike someone else, never us.

Not only were schools shut tight until the danger had passed, young people's gathering places were swept up in the mood of caution and apprehension that gripped parents and others responsible for children's activities. Officially, some pallid efforts were made for us to pursue our studies at home but since there was no compulsion and because the new school year had barely begun, one merely extended the summer holidays as completely as the polio scare would permit.

The spooky thing about it all was that nobody knew the cause of polio. It seemed to strike without discrimination or pattern, logic or reason. We learned that so-and-so had "got polio" right out of the blue, but that was that. Indeed it was a very impersonal thing until the eldest of two daughters of very close friends of our family arrived home from school one afternoon complaining of a strange stiffness in one arm. They had moved from Calgary to the simpler life of a small town of about five hundred people. Anyone who has lived in a little community knows the closeness of contacts in that particular way of life.

Barb was the first among the town's school-age youngsters to be diagnosed as a polio victim. The scary part was that the entire school population drank the same water from the town well, walked the same streets to and from class, bit the same dusty air on a windy day, touched the same books, and ate food bought at the same two stores.

The town parents, like those in the city, lived a day at a time in dreadful apprehension that their home would be visited next by the vicious disease. But the incongruous part was that Barb was the town's only polio-stricken child in the history of the place. As the weeks and years rolled by the community's fear of polio dimmed very little, for presumably the "ingredients" of infection always lurked nearby.

Barb, along with many others in this part of Alberta, became a patient at the Crippled Children's Hospital in the lower Mount Royal district of Calgary. There, minutely scrutinized by the Red Cross staff for clues, and painstakingly shielded from others, she suffered portions of her body to be operated on where muscles were thought to have shrivelled. So little was known of treatment, let alone cause, and Barb emerged a great many months later, misshapen for life by this monstrous and mysterious ailment. There was no vaccine, nothing but therapeutic exercise as a combatant, yet Barb's sister and brothers, relatives, schoolmates, and most intimate friends were untouched by polio.

My sister was believed to be out of danger, far from Alberta at university and a summer job. I, because my parents believed escape to be a sensible course of

Students of South Calgary High School have their photo taken outside King Edward School, which, for about five years during the 1920s, housed both King Edward Public School elementary students, as well as high school classes. During several of these years a poliomyelitis epidemic struck Calgary youngsters. Since it was commonly believed that overcrowded classrooms contributed to the polio outbreaks, parents were relieved when a new Western Canada High School was built in 1930, thereby reducing the number of students at King Edward. Courtesy Glenbow-Alberta Institute/NA–2517–5

action, was spirited out of town to a picturesque setting at the north end of Turner Valley not far east of the settlement of Millarville.

My determined and imaginative father assigned me the job of cooking for one of his construction crews. I had my Boy Scout cook's badge and a bit of a flair for kitchen work but never had I been the victim of a press gang manoeuvre that cast me in the role of cook in an outdoor kitchen catering to the needs of half a dozen ravenous house and barn builders. In those days of dirt and gravel roads, commuting between Calgary and the job was completely impractical. So, following instructions, I quite timidly tackled this unexpected alternative to being exposed to polio in town.

With the assistance of a couple of crew members, a kitchen was formed by smoothing a length of the steep bank of the creek and then placing the coal and wood stove at the foot of this earthen wall. Out from the bank we fashioned two low plank walls, then spread a broad canvas out over it all, attached to a pair of free-standing, tall wooden poles. So I had a reasonably high and roomy kitchen with an earthen rear wall, two wooden sides, and an open front that sloped to the edge of the creek.

The men knocked together a sturdy dining table flanked by benches and placed it firmly nearby. Using boxes and scrap lumber from the job, I made shelves along the wooden walls upon which I piled well-sealed tins and jars of foodstuffs. Out beyond the kitchen area I dug into the bed of Three Point Creek and lowered a very large metal tub into the icy water that flowed through the excavation. So there I had a natural cooler for the perishables, dry in the tub yet chilled by the fast-flowing stream.

Fortunately the weather was perfect and there was never more than a gentle breeze for the entire month I was there. Wild berries were plentiful; dairy items and vegetables were available at a farm a short walk from the creek. My accommodation was a nearby tent, shared with my father. The construction crew appeared to thrive on my cooking. As they cleaned up everything I placed before them, my courage grew to the point where I tried such dishes as saskatoon berry pie and stuffed pork chops.

Periodically I drove the elderly little Model T Ford truck into Turner Valley for supplies. On my return I would shut down its engine at the top of the embankment and make a number of trips on foot down to the kitchen with armloads of groceries.

Once, though, Father hollered to me as I drove past the job site that he wanted the truck returned in a hurry. Aiming to please, I left the engine idling while I hustled the supplies down to the kitchen. If you have ever driven a Model T you will remember its incurable and affectionate habit of nuzzling you despite your care in reefing back the brake handle to the last position on the floor ratchet. This time was no exception.

As I carried groceries down the slope beyond the edge of the kitchen, something made me look back at the chugging truck that should have been standing where I left it. Ever so slowly, it was following me. In a panic I flung the groceries away and dove at the truck's running board as it drew alongside me. I wound up with my feet waving in the air and my head down near the floor while I flailed for the handbrake or the ignition switch.

But I was too late. Upended, but fully aware of what was happening, I felt the truck crest the cutbank and launch itself out onto the canvas kitchen "roof." With a rending of fabric, we thumped down beside the stove, at which point the engine sighed and was silent.

Dinner was late that evening. The truck, the stove, and I were none the worse for the experience but my teenage dignity was as shattered as the kitchen shelves. Still, I was rather sad when news arrived a few days later that the polio risk was considered over for another year and that all schools were about to reopen. From chef to student—I considered that to be quite a comedown!

Radio's "Voice of the Prairies"

When Calgary was very young a community called Rouleauville abutted its southern edge beyond Seventeenth Avenue, then called Notre Dame. At the southwest corner of the area, by the foot of Hillcrest Avenue that winds down from Mount Royal to Mission, stands an old house that today is the Scottish Nursing Home.

A few of us remember it as having been a radio station, the home of the "Voice of the Prairies," CFCN, owned and run by a local electronics genius, W.W. Grant. An ex-navy man, inventor of a submarine detection device, and a veteran of World War I, Grant had operated an air force radio receiving station at the patrol base on the eastern outskirts of High River.

Then, having designed and built his own transmitting equipment, Grant began broadcasting words and music. His station's voice, next heard briefly from Morley, then from Calgary, became known among the continent's small but growing band of local and distant listeners.

Those were the days of negligible electronic clutter, so the Calgary station was heard with considerable clarity and regularity as far away as New York City, where one of our local programmes achieved unexpected notoriety.

A New York newspaper cartoonist by the name of Payne began picking up broadcasts in the deep of night that really tickled his funny bone. It was cowboy music from some very far-off place named Calgary, Canada, played by some whooping and hollering musicians calling themselves the Bronco Busters.

Here at home we knew who they were and who we were, but little did we know Payne was cashing in on his amusement by cartooning in the daily press the imaginary capers of the Bronco Busters away out west on the TS Ranch. He didn't know it but the letters T.S. were said to mean "The Stampede" and, in their weekly shows, the musicians made sure every listener to their broadcasts believed the music actually originated in a ranch house.

The Bronco Busters's theme was "Turkey in the Straw" played and sung with these words:

> O I come from the country where the Chinook winds blow,
> From the foothills city in the valley of the Bow,
> Where the clear, cool waters from the mountains flow,
> And the handsome women and the big men grow.

And down at the end of the rather raucous theme that went on from there, were words like this:

> Ride 'em cowboy, let 'er buck!
> We're the Bronco Busters from the valley of the Bow,
> Rum tiddle tum, tum,
> Yip! Yip!

Jack Bullough, a pianist and the musical director at the Grand Theatre, wrote the theme and many other numbers in the orchestra's original range music repertoire. He was nicknamed "The Badger" on the broadcasts. Harry Hutchcroft, another composer and performer, was known to the audiences as Bridle Bill. Shorty, who was Wally Braley, and Josh Henthorn, whose foghorn

W.W. Grant was a self-taught electronics genius. After serving during World War I in U.S. submarines, he was placed in charge of wireless services for Alberta's forestry air patrol, based in High River and Morley. Besides building and operating commercial radio stations, Bill Grant mass-produced a small, simple radio receiver under the trade name "Voice of the Prairies," soon found in nearly every farmhouse. In his later years he supervised construction of the CBC's Alberta super transmitter at Lacombe, then was engaged in the design and construction of the CBC international service's shortwave multistation array on the Tantramar Marshes in New Brunswick. CBC International Service, W.A. Nichols, "Canada's Loudest Voice," New World Illustrated, 1945

voice used to amuse and inform the grandstand crowd at the Stampede, were two more members of the Bronco Busters along with Tom Smith, who carried the name Cy Ebenezer. Many of the names, such as Curley Nixon and Slim McMurray, stuck even after the group's show was changed to "Cy Ebenezer and the Kid," then to "The Old Timers Show" that also arose from the same spirited heiferdust of the original series that ended in 1924.

Those were maverick days in radio, for it was a new medium, almost unfettered by those eager to regulate it as soon as they could manage to fathom its potential.

Somewhere along the way the Bronco Busters performed from under the roof of the King George, later the Carleton, Hotel opposite the Palliser. As part of the atmosphere the musicians had one of those noisemakers that would imitate the mooing of a cow.

On one occasion their exuberance spawned a stunt that sort of backfired. They spirited a live cow by elevator to the studio atop the hotel, where she added the most authentic atmosphere including an editorial comment on the quality of the show. She left her personal opinion embedded in the carpet!

Bill Grant, realizing the station's own originations were reaching across the continent, devised an ingenious scheme to enrich his shoestring operation's efforts to entice listeners. He installed a powerful radio receiver of his own design down in the Lethbridge area. Then, relying upon the naiveté of the telephone company's personnel, who also were groping in the new wilderness of tele-electronics, he "piped" the shows pulled in off the air in the quiet countryside, by telephone line to Calgary. Here, he rebroadcast them on his beloved CFCN. Those were Depression years, when entertainment was too costly for most people and radio offered a salvation during the days and evenings of discouraging boredom.

To ensure that people heard the broadcasts Grant designed and marketed very successful, simple, small, and cheap "Voice of the Prairies" receiving sets. The whole venture, so typical of Bill Grant's enterprise and imagination, included the excising of U.S. sponsor's commercial messages from the programs he picked up from network transmitters in Denver and Salt Lake City. Listeners to the Calgary station heard such famous pioneer radio programmes as "Lum and Abner," "Amos and Andy," "Myrt and Marge," and the singing duo Billy Jones and Ernie Hare, all sponsored by Calgary merchants! It was not until federal authorities caught up with the caper that we early Calgary listeners had to return to searching the dial for the shows we'd come to follow faithfully as local presentations.

The self-effacing local radio wizard, W.W. Grant, had set a pattern whetting our international listening appetite that persists to this day.

Noah's Ark on Rails

*I*n a 1912 newspaper editorial Calgarians read these words: "We like its mellow foghorn, its bells and its earthquake effects as it meanders up and down the street . . . " The affection was aimed at that remarkable vehicle of those days, the streetcar, and the new heavy-footed, ponderous queen of Calgary's tram fleet became variously known as the Rubberneck Car, the Sightseeing Car or, as we preferred to call it, the Scenic Car.

The garish vehicle made its first run, in a thirty-year career, on Thursday 4 July 1912. It was an early evening trip from the fairgrounds at Victoria Park to East Calgary, then out west around the Hillhurst loop, back over the old iron Louise Bridge, through town to the exhibition grounds.

Upon its arrival on a railway flatcar from its Preston, Ontario, builder, the Scenic Car had been assembled at the Victoria Park car barns. Running gear, air brakes, a front fender we always called a cow-catcher, and a rear-mounted trolley pole, were installed. The tram, over fourteen yards in length, carried fifty passengers on wooden slat seats tiered from the front to the back under metal arches supporting a striped canvas top with a scalloped fringe.

The nose of the Scenic Car added great flair to its lines, for it resembled a section of chamber pot, bulbous and generously rimmed! In the centre of it was a big, bold headlight and the entire tram, after dark, was outlined by 178 coloured lights.

From the height of the rearmost tier of seats a steep shiplike staircase descended to a semicircular rear platform, the point of exit for passengers at the end of each trip.

The car was enamelled shiny white with pinstriping of red and gold. The railings, gates, and fittings were of polished bronze and along each side of the car were seven bevel-edged plate glass mirrors starting small at the front and reaching very large proportions at the tall back end of the car. Those, for us children, were an utter joy, for if the Scenic Car paused during its ramblings we could see ourselves in the big spotless mirrors and make silly grotesque gestures before the street reflection, and ours, moved on.

The purpose of the Scenic Car was clearly stated on the flared front in big gold letters: "Seeing Calgary," and the price of the one-hour trip was 25¢.

On occasion the colourful vehicle was assigned special duty, such as that of "flagship" of a fleet of regular streetcars and their trailers that hauled large groups of picnickers on summer outings to local parks. In that treasure house of Glenbow is a photo of the Scenic Car leading a flotilla to Bowness in 1915, its mirrors masked by big banners proclaiming "Hudson's Bay A.A.A Field Day."

A very famous Scenic Car pose (included here) was taken on its first week in service in 1912 while it paused for passengers to view the breathtaking spectacle of downtown Calgary. The spot was on the hillside ledge that once sloped rather precariously from a low point in Sunnyside up the North Hill escarpment to join Centre Street at the north end of the bridge.

When that photo was taken the tall, outstanding structures in and near the core of town seen from that eyrie were the Palliser Hotel, the Grain Exchange and Lancaster Buildings, McDougall

The Scenic Car made its first sightseeing trip on 4 July 1912. Built by the Preston Car and Coach Company of Ottawa, it carried the Calgary crest, the number 50, and the words "Seeing Calgary" in gold lettering on its bulbous white prow. On each side, beneath seven bronze railings, were seven mirror panels of British bevelled plate glass. The Calgary Herald, in an editorial, said the car looked "something like Noah's ark on a trip to Fairyland." Courtesy Glenbow-Alberta Institute / NA–2553–4

School, in those days the Normal School, and a slender brick chimney that towered above the railway heating plant and the roofline of the hotel.

Still, it was a panorama shown visitors with pride in those days when streetcars were the chief mode of getting out to see the place, for Calgary was getting big! It had a population of fifty thousand, about three hundred miles of graded roads and, at night, a panoply of as many as five hundred street lights!

The Scenic Car itself was almost a suburb of lights silhouetted, as it was, in coloured bulbs. After dark and by daylight the tram carried, on average, about thirty thousand sightseers each season on its hour-long jaunts.

Its base was Centre Street on the south side of the Mall intersection where, today, it would park with its back to the Calgary Tower. By 1919, with streetcar routes expanded up the hills into some of the residential districts, the Scenic Car was placed on a summer schedule of six trips daily with departures between 10 A.M. and 9 P.M.

There was a cruise through the industrialized part of East Calgary. Another trip stopped at the city's high point, Twenty-sixth Avenue and Twentieth Street SW, which, back then, provided passengers with an unobstructed view of the city on both sides of the Bow River as well as a westward sweep of the Rockies.

A popular daily jaunt took sightseers along both rivers, looping through Elbow Park and Sunnyside, when the rivers were not in flood, of course! "Eighteen miles of western scenery along the Bow River" was an evening favourite under the striped canopy and amid the coloured lights, for the car became a regular warm weather visitor to Bowness Park.

It's something I remember clearly from my younger days: the tram growling past at low speed, the tiered sightseers holding their hats and squinting their eyes against the dusty wind that thought-lessly whistled through. Up front, the driver, in his navy blue uniform with gold braid, was hunching over the brass controls. Behind him, facing the slope of filled seats, the similarly clad conductor was bellowing through his megaphone the highlights and secrets that comprised the enchantment of a view of Calgary from the Scenic Car.

Put 'er There, Partner

A few of our pioneers appeared content to "go it alone," each carving his own niche in the western emptiness. But man, being a gregarious animal, has always been more inclined to seek a partner, and so it was with most of our settlers.

Partnership, stormy or peaceful, romantic or commercial, in story as well as reality, is not limited to Cain and Abel, salt and pepper, Romeo and Juliet, fish and chips, David and Goliath, ham and eggs, or even Huntley and Palmer. A great deal of Calgary was built upon partnerships and one might wonder how the two came together. Was it a dream-sharing, or simply economics? How difficult was it to decide who got top billing?

A good Calgary example is the Leeson-Lineham Block that still stands staunchly on Stephen Avenue opposite The Bay. George K. Leeson was one of the mail contractors who, with team and coach, carried the mail to and from Calgary in days gone by. He was a rancher, too, and a partner in the province's first oil-well firm, the Rocky Mountain Development Company.

John Lineham also was a cattleman, and investor in that pioneer Waterton oil drilling venture at Oil City. That was enough to propel them into sharing the cost of a "towering" six-storey brick and sandstone downtown office building that turned out to be just one of Leeson's many very successful Calgary real estate ventures.

Among the tenants of the Leeson-Lineham Block was a real estate team that included a former Maritimer, H.A. Burgess, and N.B. Moss, who was born and raised at Calgary Junction. They summarized their mutual business philosophy by saying, "It has been proven beyond all question that real estate offers the safest investment that can be made. There are many reasons for this, chief among which is that holdings of dirt cannot be stolen or run away."

Another safe business venture was the recession-proof field of foodstuffs. George W. Thornton and H. Lloyd Jackson, a pair from Perth, Ontario, set up shop here in 1912 and soon had a thriving retail trade in staple and fancy groceries, teas, coffees, spices, vegetables, and fruits. Soon their volume of business required them to add to their in-house sales staff, as well as hire two drivers, horse teams, and a pair of wagons to handle their customer home-delivery service.

On the lighter side of Calgary life, the firm of Young and Kennedy supplied the more wealthy citizens with sheet music, pianos, and musical instruments, as well as a new musical gadget called a phonograph or gramophone or, its trade name—Victrola—which played records. Years ago D.J. Young told me that away back then if they had not sold one of those music-makers, valued at about $1,000, by noon, he and Kennedy labelled it a slow day!

Arising from the nonfrivolous side of early Calgary business were the teams of Mackay and Dippie on Eighth Avenue a few doors west of the Hudson's Bay store, and of Simpson and Lea on Centre Street between Seventh and Eighth avenues. Both pairs of merchants dealt directly with trappers and tanners in raw and dressed skins. They handled furs, hides and, in the case of the former pair, taxidermy, sporting goods, firearms, Indian curios, and tailored "fine furs for ladies."

A couple of Calgary teams did a large business in dairy products. K.A. Andersen and Berg Pallesen home-delivered milk,

cream, buttermilk, and cheese throughout the small city from their own dairy northwest of Calgary. Another, specializing in ice cream, was Campbell and Griffin, whose cold storage and other facilities were located on Eleventh Avenue near Fourth Street West, formerly the site of the first home my father built for himself and his newly arrived bride in 1906.

Speaking of "former," one other recession-proof business was that of funeral directors. Predominant in the field during Calgary's early days was the team of Graham and Buscombe, located on Centre Street at Seventh Avenue. J.K. Buscombe, a Hamilton casket manufacturer by trade, went into partnership in 1905 with Ontario-born A.C. Graham, a realtor and former Winnipeg tailor. Their funeral and embalming business offered customers such choices as horse-drawn or motorized hearses with bevelled-glass windows and, if a late Calgarian's survivors so wished, a matching team of white or black horses.

The small city had a lion's share of enterprising partnerships, including brokers and commission agents McKelvie and Stirrett; photographers and picture framers E. Bailey and E.N. Grant; realtors galore, including Baldwin and Ruttle, and Rogers and Wright (a team of former plough company salesmen from New York and Alberta). There were also Calgary old-timers who came here when the settlement clustered around Fort Calgary—Pinkham and Macleod, the latter being Norman, son of Colonel Macleod, who named Calgary.

"Harnessed in commerce," these are only a sampling of the pairs who, early in this century, shaped the business pattern of Calgary during the formative phase of its early years.

Opposite: *Partnerships, so important in the early stages of Calgary's commercial development, extended well beyond retail or wholesale businesses and many professions. Even a small city's policemen needed reliable workmates, both man and beast. This quartet of horsemen constables, astride rented mounts, proved the value of close partnership when the policemen tested and successfully used the horses for crowd control and patrol duties in 1910 and 1911.* Courtesy Glenbow-Alberta Institute/NA–523–9

Venice of the North

*E*nglish town planner Thomas Mawson, who pictured Calgary as "the Venice of the North," wrote in his 1914 report to the city: "The parks, public gardens and playgrounds of any city must necessarily play a very large part in its civic life . . . the great thing is to make sure there will be at least one small open space within easy reach of every dwelling in the city."

Our local parks development began in 1885 when pioneer William Pearce, a dominion land surveyor, saw to it that Central Park, now Memorial Park, was set aside in a federal land gift to the city as a perpetual midtown park. Our first real children's playgrounds appear to have been established in 1907, when the city population of 21,000 included about 3,300 youngsters beneath the age of fourteen. St. George's Island was still a fairly primitive midriver park where some swings were erected for the enjoyment of the little people.

Two years later playgrounds were established on school property at the East Ward, South Ward, and Central schools and the privately run Western Canada College. In that year of 1909 playgrounds were proposed at the junction of Ninth and Seventeenth avenues east, across from the brewery; Eighth Avenue and Eleventh Street East, near the St. George's Island bridge; First Street East near Fourth Avenue; the corner of Sixth Avenue West at Second Street; and two along the Bow River, at Langevin Bridge and at the Eau Clair Lumber Mill, near the Bow Marsh Bridge at Tenth Street.

The location of those playgrounds certainly indicated the size and emphasis of the little city, for the spread had not yet occurred outwards to today's Exhibition, Mewata, and Hillhurst's park areas. When that civic expansion did occur and Calgary began spreading north of the Bow River and towards the west, city council decreed that each subdivision plan had to deed at least 5 percent of its area to the city for park space. Then outlying playgrounds began appearing on the maps of expanding Calgary, such as out at Mewata, still on an outer edge of the built-up area.

The World War I years somewhat inhibited development of Calgary's playgrounds, but in 1917 the city hired its first full-time professional playground director, Muriel E. Ireland, later to become Mrs. Muriel Kerby. She had worked for five summers in Winnipeg, supervising some of their toughest playground youngsters and, immediately upon making the move to our city, shouldered the entire job because her supervisor, a YMCA worker, was leaving for overseas military duty.

Muriel Ireland tackled the big and diversified assignment with courage and determination. On 10 July 1918, nine playground centres opened in an area between St. George's Island, Mewata, Crescent Heights, and Elbow Park. Three were full-time operations, six days a week, the others were open three days weekly. Hours of operation differed from one centre to another, but together they spanned a stretch from 10 A.M. to 9 P.M., with the evening hours proving a magnet for the teen crowd and young people of twenty years and older.

An over-eager city council had authorized their opening a bit too soon, so three had to be closed immediately until playground equipment arrived in town. But by August 1918 team games were in full swing at all playgrounds. Round-robin competitions and interplayground rivalry became instantly popular in contests such as baseball, volleyball, dodgeball, and basketball. Audiences of as many as five hundred cheered as the teams vied for points and ribbons.

During that 1918 summer, the Victoria playground won a banner for the highest points and, as Muriel Ireland's organization improved its performance, sports efficiency standards were set, tests were held for would-be competitors, and buttons were awarded those who passed the test and thus became eligible as team and individual players.

The influenza epidemic that swept the country following World War I pulled the heady program to a reluctant halt, but when full activities returned

In this view, looking west beyond Central (Memorial) Park, the Colonel Belcher Hospital overshadows the stately sandstone home of Pat Burns. The mansion was demolished in 1956 to make room for expansion of the hospital. Central Park, renamed Memorial in 1928, never was a playground, although it was a favourite scene for band concerts. Its formal nature was emphasized in 1928 when the Federal Geodetic Authorities sank a seven-foot concrete column there as a "reference point for all precise levelling bench marks in Calgary and vicinity." The official altitude is 3,439.66 feet, or 1,048.41 metres above sea level. **Courtesy Glenbow-Alberta Institute/NA–2399–39**

Riverside won the city competition with a total of 148 efficiency button awards to its community youngsters. Plans for the following year, 1919, included integrating playground games and teamwork into school programmes. This meant the summer playground programmes were to act as a fitness "build-up" for the schools' autumn sports calendars.

One measure of the success of Muriel Ireland's first year's work was an attendance of 64,303 during the school vacation period. An indication of the young woman's public service dedication had to do with her own health. She was the city's first victim of the influenza epidemic, having contracted it through nursing a desperately ill girl on the westbound train that brought Miss Ireland here. Her patient was the sole survivor of that family and Ireland, in turn, was nursed by Dr. C.S. Mahood, alongside whom she later worked in the Stampede Days' emergency hospital. She held the St. John Ambulance Honour Certificates in first aid and in nursing. So upon her swift recovery and during the temporary closure of playgrounds due to the epidemic, she was able to put her nursing skills to good Samaritan use.

Letterhead dated 23 July 1918 reveals the Calgary Playgrounds Association to have been located in the old YWCA, 223 Twelfth Avenue SW. Mrs. Harold Riley was the group's president and its secretary was Dr. Mahood. It was under the aegis of William R. Reader, superintendent of playgrounds for the city, and Muriel Ireland had the quaint title of superintendent of supervision.

A small folder, tawny with age, listing the 1918 Inter-playground Competition under the city's auspices, charts the contests for 8, 13, and 15 August, culminating in the Annual Playground Field Day on St. George's Island, Thursday, 22 August: "An attractive program of folk dances, song and ring games, team games and athletics will be given."

In the athletic finals prior to that season's wind-up in the island park, youngsters were graded by body weight, A being "65 lbs. and under," and E "over 110 lbs." Competitions were slated in "Playground Ball, Basketball, Volley Ball, Dodge Ball, Football, and Track and Field Athletics." Division A grouped Mewata Park, Riley Park, and Crescent Heights playgrounds. Division B consisted of St. George's Island, Riverside, Ramsay, and Victoria. Games were scheduled to start at 7:15 on the evening of 15 August at Victoria playground.

Throughout the summer, before these big events took place, youngsters, in their own home areas, practised to achieve efficiency and to win the coveted playground efficiency button. Proudly wearing that emblem of achievement, they converged upon the Victoria playground, in those days the hub of that sort of activity. In that year of 1918, Muriel Ireland, on behalf of her hardworking playground teams, stated the program's purpose in these words: "To have every boy and girl who is a member of a playground take part in this test so that they may have the opportunity of contributing 'their little mite' for their playground."

When Corporal Johnny Came Limping Home

*I*n 1914, tears, born of tragedy, pity, and pain, were being shed upon the arrival in Calgary of most passenger trains from the east. World War I was in progress and aboard these trains were local young men wounded on the European battlefields. Willing arms welcomed and tenderly helped them complete the long and painful trip from wartorn France and Belgium out to the Ogden military hospital at the southeast corner of the city.

It was Alberta's first military convalescent hospital, established by the Alberta Red Cross Society with the blessing of the country's military hospital commission. At first, the society's aim was to minister to the needs of army personnel who were training locally at Sarcee Camp and Victoria Park. Soon it became apparent there was a much larger role to be played, for war casualties requiring immediate care began to arrive during the first months of the overseas conflict.

The three-storey, stone-trimmed red brick building stood at the entrance to the huge Ogden railway shops. It had been the Ogden Hotel, built primarily to cater to visiting railway company officials. It was quite imposing, with white pillars along a sort of C-shaped ground level veranda and another, also out front, on the floor above. The lobby had become a sitting room and reception area, backed by a staircase of polished dark wood leading up to former hotel rooms, now patient wards, and an operating room.

The philanthropy of A.E. Cross, famous as one of the "Big Four" of the Calgary Stampede, and head of the Calgary Brewery, had made this one of his firm's hotels available to the Red Cross volunteers. Before it was taken out of service in 1919 it, and a small annex down the slope to the south on Ogden Road, ministered to the needs of as many as 270 battle casualties at a time.

As a youngster I was occasionally permitted—if I agreed to behave and not make a noise—to accompany my mother, who frequently visited the returned men, as they were known, to bring them reading material, snacks, and a good measure of encouragement for speedy recoveries.

I, of course, was admonished to remain in the main entry area where I fidgeted between bouts of tears over something very adult that my childish logic was too immature to comprehend. On earlier visits to Sarcee Camp, where thousands of troops under canvas trained for armed combat, I had seen the camp mascot, a live and bewildered bear cub, wearing a collar and chain, usually clinging to an old tree stump set into the ground near the parade square.

Now, no more than a few months later, that same bear cub, immortalized by a taxidermist, clung to an artificial stump affixed to the newel post of the staircase and gazed with brown glass eyes at the dreary hotel scene. A knot of sympathetic nurses, and soldiers on crutches, tried hard to explain how much happier the bear cub was in the hospital than out at the camp. Unconsoled, I decided war was a bad thing, especially hard on bears.

When the Ogden hospital closed its doors its patients were moved to the Sunnyside Infirmary on Eighth Avenue NW in Hillhurst. Since 1911 that odd-looking structure, now replaced by part of Grace Hospital in the lee of the hill, had been an Anglican

Church place of learning—the Bishop Pinkham School for Boys. As a military hospital it had a lifespan of only three years because a new facility for veterans had been established closer to town.

This first Colonel Belcher Hospital was in a converted brick warehouse once belonging to the Fairbanks Morse heavy machinery firm. Today it is Penny Lane on Eighth Avenue SW, seemingly a most unlikely location for a 135-bed military hospital. But there, conveniently if somewhat noisily fronted by streetcar lines used by its visitors, it served battlefield casualties for seven years. Then it moved, but only two doors to the east and still on the outskirts of downtown Calgary, for, in those days, there were no shops other than corner groceries west of Third Street!

The final move came when the present Colonel Belcher Hospital was opened on the site of the stately Pat Burns sandstone mansion in its beautiful city-block-sized garden. Even in these days, well beyond the hospital's strictly military role, the name of the establishment honours a warrior. The proper name of the Eighth Avenue West facility was the Alberta Military Hospital but the public preferred the colloquial Colonel Belcher title.

Lieutenant-Colonel Robert Belcher, C.M.G., who was born in England, began his military career with the mounted police at Fort Garry in 1873. He was transferred to Fort Macleod and, in 1875, was here during the building of Fort Calgary.

Belcher's steady climb through the ranks found him as inspector in May 1897, assigned to London during Queen Victoria's jubilee celebrations. The winters of 1897 and 1898 were spent in command of a detachment at Chilkoot Pass during the Yukon gold rush. The force put his experience to good use later at Dawson City, Bonanza, and El Dorado during those restless, rough and tumble times of gold fever.

Robert Belcher was second in command of "Strathcona's Horse," the outfit whose recruiting headquarters was the Fort Calgary barracks of the mounted police, from whose ranks most of its members volunteered for military service in the South African war. Major Belcher was mentioned in dispatches and awarded the Order of St. Michael and St. George for his distinguished campaigning.

He also participated in overseas warfare during World War I from 1914 to 1918 as colonel of the Nineteenth Alberta Dragoons, capping thirty-three years of mounted police service. Unfortunately Colonel Belcher did not live long enough to take part in the ceremonies marking the opening of the hospital bearing his name. He died in 1919.

Opposite: *Built in 1913 and still standing at the entrance to the CPR Ogden Shops, this building served as a hotel for visiting CPR officials. During World War I, the Red Cross Society used it as a hospital for wounded armed forces men just returned from battlefields overseas. Red Cross nurses, army doctors, and ambulatory patients posed in the afternoon sunshine for this portrait in 1917. Courtesy* Glenbow-Alberta Institute/NA–1195–1

Picture Perfect Pollard

Calgary's most widely travelled citizen came west in 1899 from his birthplace of Tillsonburg, Ontario, and before long the Harry Pollard Photographic Studio in the Tribune Block on Stephen Avenue was a very busy place in the town of forty thousand.

Pollard learned his profession at an early age from his father, James Pollard, who had apprenticed in England and was highly regarded in southern Ontario for the artistic and mechanical excellence of his daguerreotype and tintype photos. Young Pollard brought those, and more modern skills, with him and, after a devastating fire in 1906 in which he lost most of his negatives, he started anew with the latest equipment, a sumptuously appointed studio, and a burning desire to broaden his horizons and accept new challenges.

He first encountered Alberta Indians in 1904 when he won their confidence at Sun Dance ceremonies south of Cluny. His tripod-mounted 8 x 10 black camera and his need to duck under a black cloth to take the pictures caused considerable apprehension but, over the years, Pollard amassed a collection of about two hundred portraits of Indian chiefs.

In those days before the invention of colour film, Harry tinted many of his Indian portraits by hand. He entrusted scenic view colouring to a Mrs. C.F. Adams, but always did the Indian head studies himself. An exhibit of their tinted work was placed on show during Stampede Week years ago in the windows of Eaton's new store. The display included spectacular mountain views in addition to portraits of Blackfoot Chief Calf Child, the Blood's Martin Horses, and Rough Hair—a Stoney.

Harry Pollard had developed another western love, the mountains. He photographed a month-long journey from Field to Jasper in company with Canadian and United States wilderness buffs who had the aid of sixty-four pack and saddle ponies! He became a very accomplished mountaineer. With Calgary companions T.B. Moffat, M.D. Geddes, and guide Conrad Kain he lugged his 5 x 7 plate camera, black headcloth, and all necessary gear to the peak of 12,972-foot Mount Robson on the second expedition to conquer Canada's highest peak. Fired by this success, Pollard added many more vertical miles to his travels by scaling, and photographing on the way up and down, 11,870-foot Mount Assiniboine and nearly twenty other Alberta and British Columbia peaks such as Mount Stephen, Cathedral, Temple, and Victoria and, with the inevitable camera, every peak surrounding Banff.

Harry Pollard's love affair with the mountains paid dividends in notoriety, for the cherubic-faced, happy little man, astride a rather primitive motorcycle with sidecar, became the first motorized Calgarian to make it to Banff when the road was very little more than a rocky track. Aboard a Pierce Arrow car fitted with train wheels, he travelled the narrow gauge White Pass and Yukon Route taking photos all the way. Harry Pollard, Jr., at the wheel of the family Nash touring car on 9 June 1927, was the first motorist and photographer to drive the new Kicking Horse Pass road between Field and Golden.

Harry Sr. always had an instinctive sense of the immediate. When the Dingman #1 well blew in at Turner Valley in 1914, Harry and his camera were there. The morning after the fearful Turtle

When Eighth Avenue was not being used for everyday traffic, it was the route followed by every sort of parade. In this famous 1918 photograph, Pollard captured the 363rd Infantry, United States Troops marching on Canadian soil for the first time in history, during World War I. Courtesy Provincial Archives of Alberta/H. Pollard Collection/P.4058

Mountain slide at Frank, Harry was there taking pictures of the devastated scene. On 13 February 1947, when Leduc #1 heralded a new era of oil production, Pollard captured the historic sight on film.

For a few years the Pollards lived in Victoria where Harry was the western movie cameraman for Associated Screen News and Pathé News, meaning that the skill of the Calgarian was recognized far afield. He was approached by the Canadian Pacific Railway whose advertising boasted "Spans the World" and hired as official photographer on Empress liner round-the-world cruises. His first global voyage was aboard the Empress of Canada in 1924 and annually for fourteen years he circled the world aboard the Empresses of Australia, France, Canada, and Britain, sailing out of Montreal or New York. In those days a typical Empress cruise took nearly five months, covering thirty thousand miles while visiting forty-five cities in twenty countries. Passengers made many inland side-trips and, with about 320 tourists in tow, misadventures were inevitable.

Harry Pollard was arrested about six times, usually for choosing sacred or political backgrounds forbidden to visitors. He should not have photographed a camel train near the Sea of Galilee, nor the Jewish Wailing Wall and some mosques in Jerusalem. But he was allowed to be the first cameraman within the altar room of the Temple of the Emerald Buddha in Bangkok. When Egyptologist Howard Carter opened the tomb of Pharaoh Tutankhamen, Pollard was with him, later giving Carter the negatives of the photos he had taken in the chambers inside the pyramid.

As CPR cruise photographer, Harry also logged three Mediterranean and seven West Indian cruises and was aboard the Princess Norah, of the railway's west coast steamships, on her maiden voyage to Alaska with Governor General Lord Willingdon and Viscountess Willingdon as passengers. At the Banff Springs Hotel he photographed Winston Churchill and crossed Canada as photographer of the Duke of Gloucester's party in the 1920s. After his tens of thousands of miles that included five round trips across Canada, Harry Pollard felt he had been everywhere, saying, "For all that it is round, the world's flat." He added, "Calgary is the best spot on earth I know of."

It was at his Calgary studio in 1908 that Harry Pollard met Eleanor Tillen, who had come to Calgary from her hometown of Rainy River in 1898 to live with an aunt. Such was her beauty that in 1908 Ella was crowned Miss Canada and led the Dominion Fair Parade that year at the age of eighteen. In 1911 she became Mrs. Pollard.

Two of his children, Helen and William, inherited some of the Pollard propensity for journeying. Helen's profession of arranging national and international tours for senior citizens, she once admitted, drastically cut back her travelling and skiing miles. When I spoke with her in 1985, she pinpointed for me some bright highlights of her father's career. He was especially proud of the portraits of his close friends, cowboy artist Charlie Russell and editor Bob Edwards. He took a superb shot of Lord Strathcona and Father Lacombe, seated, deep in conversation, and a fine hilltop view of the original Fort Calgary.

His most famous news photo was a view of the United States 363rd Infantry from Camp Lewis near Seattle (included here). On their way overseas during World War I, on 23 June 1918, the men paused for a short rest in Calgary. Marching with a band they filled Eighth Avenue between Centre and First Street West, the first United States troops to parade under arms on Canadian soil. The photo made the front pages in New York and was reproduced throughout the continent.

One of Harry Pollard's proudest achievements had nothing to do with photography. He was one of the group responsible for introducing to Alberta the wild Hungarian partridge, which, since 1908, has adapted to become one of our prized game birds.

A sentimental purchase by Harry was Castle Mountain Lodge, a mountaineering base for himself and a learning experience for his sons. In 1924 British United Press writer Don Osborne paid a most eloquent tribute to Harry Pollard: "Romance surrounds him like a cloak, history walks beside him, adventure crowds his heels."

Chinese Were Our Fellow Pioneers

*E*arly in 1879 the federal government called for construction tenders for one of the toughest sections of the proposed transcontinental railway. The successful bidder was Andrew Onderdonk, who estimated he would need about ten thousand labourers, nearly one-third of British Columbia's population, to build the Fraser Canyon stretch of track.

Once the enormously difficult construction job got underway, the exploitative contractor had to plumb whatever "dregs" of the labour pool, as he would have called them, he could find to perform the incredibly difficult and hazardous work. In 1882 and 1883 he imported Chinese labourers to work for a dollar a day, one-third less than their white counterparts. There were seventeen thousand of them and, when the dangerous job was completed, it was estimated the railway line had cost the lives of six hundred Chinese, four men for every mile of canyon track.

Eventually cast adrift, jobless in a hostile society, the Chinese well remembered their pitifully small rewards for backbreaking work and were willing to try anything to keep body and soul intact. Thus many of them made the eastward journey across the mountains, arriving almost penniless in what was to become Alberta.

Thus the Chinese in this part of Alberta came to be synony-mous with restaurants, vegetables, and laundries, their lack of sophistication proving quite acceptable in those simpler days. The federal Chinese Exclusion Law, passed in 1923 and not repealed until 1947, pleased bigots, for it meant a continuance of the ban on the Chinese right to vote, enter certain professions, and to send for their families to join them in Canada.

With traditional Oriental stoicism, scores of lone Chinese men established themselves as the sole restaurateurs in many prairie towns. Their cafes were much alike. Up front was a small glass cash counter with a display of Turret and Sweet Caporal cigarettes, Old Chum chewing tobacco, Peg Top cigars, and Wrigley's gum. Deeper into the building a high lunch counter, with a row of disc-topped swivel stools, extended along one wall. Along the other were partitioned booths, possibly with a sign stating "Booths for Ladies" to encourage unescorted women to dine sheltered from uninvited distractions.

The kitchen was beyond a pair of port-holed swinging doors through which was fetched, by an unsmiling Chinese, the basic, substantial fare that epitomized The City Cafe, Kwong's Cafe, The Club Cafe, or the Railway Cafe. Despite the lack of today's gleaming food preparation areas, Hoy Chong's or Chan Lee's seemed to dispense nourishment with precious little customer indigestion or stomach upset. For ex-railway builders the Chinese cafe cooks proved capable of turning out remarkably good pastry and could have given lessons to today's pizza "cooks" who appear to have a pact with BC's plywood manufacturers!

The Chinese restaurant menu was simple, perhaps saving the proprietor from having to expand his culinary skill or, more vitally, his knowledge of our difficult language: breaded veal cutlets, hot beef sandwich, sausage, pork chops, ham and eggs, mashed potatoes, rice pudding, raisin pie, apple pie, milk, and coffee. It was

The Chinese who settled on the Prairies in the wake of their railway-building work established themselves as restaurateurs, household servants, vegetable sellers, and laundrymen. They were trustworthy and hard-working, and they carefully preserved their ethnic identity. Here, during the 1920s, a city development made it necessary for this Chinese family to move its laundry business and relocate as a useful and valued part of another Calgary neighbourhood. Courtesy Glenbow-Alberta Institute/NA–2186–33

good basic food that successfully nourished thousands of us in years past.

When Calgary was quite small, rows of suburban homes were easily reached by the Chinese vegetable man, who appeared when the spring weather began to warm, and who seemed to hibernate with the onslaught of the frosts. One of them came along our street every week without fail. A rather woebegone horse pulled his equally elderly black cart while he walked alongside watching for housewives, who, upon his approach, would scurry out to stop him and check his wares.

In the cool gloom of the cart would be banks of vegetables and fruits, all glistening fresh. Weigh scales, like those of "The Scales of Justice," were near the open side of the cart. From the end of the cross-arm opposite the various weights was suspended, on little chains, a metal bowl shaped like a half-walnut in which the purchases were placed to be weighed and priced.

The Chinese vegetable man's English was skimpy but his measurements of purchases were always generous. The elderly man who cruised Twenty-eighth Street had a complexion like parchment. He never would have made our list of the ten best-dressed men, but he had a smile worth a million, enhanced by a mouthful of gleamy teeth that were mostly silver and gold. That, he saved for his shy gift of a handful of litchi nuts reserved for favourite regular customers.

Mother was a steady patron and, each spring, the vegetable man, grinning metallically, would slip her a lily bulb that she would prop in water among stones gathered from the back garden path. It seemed each year the lily bloomed promptly at Easter as though in league with the calendar.

Also found in the city in those days was the typical Chinese laundry, a little clapboard building with a clattering front door that opened close to a counter worn smooth by the handing back and forth of many bundles. On it, at one end, was a spike bearing a column of little newsprint-quality paper squares that sagged a bit in the steamy, quite fragrant air of the little place.

Beyond a door, a room at the back looked brighter than the "office," with its single, naked light globe. You could see laundry tubs on a stove that glowed dull red in spots. Black smoothing irons stood heating on the iron stove-top. A hand-cranked wringer or mangle loomed amid baskets and tubs and a cloud of steam.

The atmosphere of the Chinese laundry is not as memorable as the business of it. As soon as you presented your newsprint-paper ticket the proprietor would lift down, from among seemingly identical parcels that lined much of the wall behind the counter, none other than your laundry. Each stack of packages was smoothly wrapped in blank newsprint paper and tied with white cotton string. The only identification was a brushed Chinese symbol on a square of paper, the incomprehensible mark matching your own.

Shirts were meticulously pressed and folded, as was every garment, pillowcase, and sheet. The price was murmured in very bad English. Nobody ever seemed to haggle over price, nobody questioned honesty or linen count or damage, for it was an honourable transaction between honourable people. In cultural terms, those Chinese who kept some of us fed, and those who kept many of us clean, were centuries removed from their homeland and from the servitude-like railway work that had brought them among us. Many had cheated death on the Fraser Canyon cliffs, others had survived some ugly episodes of racial intolerance in Alberta communities. Then, at last, a new chapter opened for them and their descendants when immigration regulations were relaxed somewhat, and as Pacific Rim nations began, in peace time, to regard one another with increased respect and tolerance.

The "Big Four" Plus One

When Calgary was still quite tiny a few ranchers who had settled several miles to the south in the Fish Creek Valley formed an agricultural society. In 1897 they held a one-day fair with foot and horse races; a brag or two in the form of displaying prized livestock, flowers, and vegetables; and a bake sale, accompanied by a lot of neighbourliness in that year of Queen Victoria's diamond jubilee.

In 1851 Queen Victoria had opened the garish Crystal Palace in London, recognizing the wonderful progress of the nineteenth century. So the people of the British Empire were in an exhibition, as well as a party, mood that continued as long as people of the colonies and dominions were bedazzled by the glories of the Victorian era.

Far-off Calgary took part in the protracted salutes to national and international pride, to industry, prosperity, and growth. Our Victoria Day parades moved along bunting-bedecked streets and then, when King George V succeeded to the throne, even more celebrations were triggered. Singing children, Indians in full regalia, cowboys and cowgirls, ranchers, and decorated industrial floats made up a parade of four thousand marchers trudging between Mewata Park and Victoria Park past an onlooking and cheering throng of thirty thousand.

Those were the beginnings of today's parade and exhibition.

At this same time there was a feeling in the United States that the traditions and cowboy skills of the West were disappearing before the onrush of settlement across hitherto ranching country. Young Guy Weadick of Rochester, New York, shared the belief. While still a teenager, he headed west to learn to be a rider and fancy roper.

In 1905 Weadick and a little troupe of performing cowboys put on a show here adjacent to our fifth annual Inter-Western Pacific Exhibition. While here he met a far-sighted Canadian Pacific Railway livestock agent, H.C. McMullen, who willingly listened to Weadick's enthusiastic pitch for an annual western rodeo show. Weadick felt Calgary was an ideal base for a performance like that but McMullen believed we were not yet ready for it.

Crestfallen, Weadick continued his troupe's barnstorming across the continent and put on performances as far off as England. By 1911 Weadick, now married to trick roper Flores La Due, was an accomplished performer and promoter. He was delighted to return to Calgary, which, according to McMullen, was now ready to preserve the old west by staging an annual rodeo. His search for sponsors brought him in contact with four local ranchers who agreed to back the idea, thus becoming famous as the "Big Four."

Actually a Medicine Hat rancher by the name of Day primed the pump, as it were, with $10,000 and soon George Lane, A.E. Cross, Pat Burns, and the Honourable A.J. McLean, who was Alberta's provincial secretary, had added their contributions to bring the seed money to a total of $100,000. Weadick agreed to their stipulation that the show's profits were to be donated to charity, and they told the young New Yorker that the rodeo had better be a success!

Weadick was thrilled and wasted no time trumpeting all over North America his forthcoming spectacle of a Frontier Day Celebration and Stampede. The show opened on Labour Day, 2

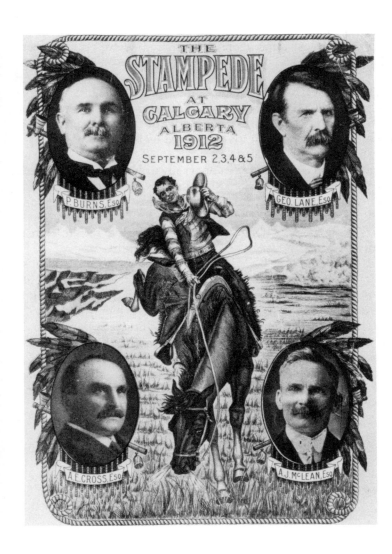

A few show-off, range riding cowboys competed on their own turf to prove who was the better rider and roper. Then along came a New York showman named Guy Weadick. He talked some local ranchers into financing and staging a public demonstration of cowpuncher skills as an added attraction to the local summer agricultural and livestock show. Now the Calgary Exhibition and Stampede, more than eighty years old, is deservedly called "The Greatest Outdoor Show on Earth." This is the front cover of the program printed for the first Stampede, held in 1912. Courtesy Glenbow-Alberta Institute/NA–604–1

September 1912, with a parade watched by sixty thousand people. The four-day event was quickly expanded to six and really set the world's press on its ear. Suddenly our Calgary Exhibition, because it was fired by an outstanding rodeo, became world famous.

World War I intervened, halting the annual performance until 1919, when Guy Weadick was brought back to Calgary by the Big Four to stage a victory stampede a month after the victory exhibition. Both were rousing successes. In 1923 the two events were married, with Weadick named manager of the rodeo. The Calgary Exhibition and Stampede was born.

Needless to say the Big Four were delighted that their faith in Weadick and his idea was justified. Today they are well remembered by the large and unusual building that bears their name. On the exhibition grounds, now called Stampede Park, were a pair of one-storey exhibition halls known as the Bessborough and the Willingdon buildings, named after two of our governors general. The buildings stood side by side with their backs to the Macleod Trail until they were given a new chapter in life by being moved east of the Elbow River as backstage rodeo facilities.

On the site today is the two-storey Big Four Building, a year-round focal point of Stampede grounds activities, principally curling, even though, I believe, it was originally earmarked for exhibits and events such as dog shows and other specialty exhibitions. The first level was opened to the public in 1957, the second two years later. Weadick, who became an Alberta resident prior to his retirement, and the four original sponsors are commemorated there where many thousands gather each year.

Pat Burns supplied fresh meat to construction crews on the Calgary-Edmonton Railway in 1890. He parleyed the output of his first little abattoir east of the Elbow River into one of Canada's twenty-five largest corporations. He acquired twelve cattle ranches totalling some half-million acres and was appointed to the Senate in 1934.

The Honourable **Archibald J. McLean,** also Ontario-born, came west in 1881. After five years in Manitoba he became a large-scale cattle and horse rancher east of Lethbridge. McLean represented Lethbridge in the provincial legislature and was appointed provincial secretary.

Iowa-born **George Lane,** a rancher since his teen years, worked at the Bar U Ranch west of High River for seven years before joining Pat Burns's staff to feed Indians who had lost their buffalo food supply. After buying the "Flying U" west of Nanton, he established the "Y.T." horse ranch near Bassano where he raised North America's largest and finest herd of Percheron horses.

Alfred Ernest Cross, a Montrealer, acquired his veterinarian's degree there, then homesteaded on Mosquito Creek, west of Nanton. A serious illness changed the direction of his life and he learned the skills of a brewer in Montreal. Returning west in 1892 he established the Calgary Brewing and Malting Company. Cross became deeply involved in many early Calgary activities and was a director of the Western Stock Breeders' Association.

These men of vision—the Big Four Plus One—made possible The Greatest Outdoor Show on Earth: Calgary's annually burnished world crown.

Many Women Were Indeed Our "Better Halves"

*S*ome remarkable Calgary mothers lived among us and left their modest, but indelible, marks long before Mother's Day was invented to salute them.

One noteworthy pioneer was Mrs. W.S. Shaw, who arrived with her family in the Fish Creek Valley in 1883. Wife of an English chemist, she must have summoned every ounce of her courage to agree to the long trek in search of a new life on the untested Canadian frontier.

Her responsibilities were enormous, for the Shaws had eight children ranging in age from sixteen to an infant in arms. The family brought with them into the unknown enough provisions for a year. From the end of steel at Swift Current they came the rest of the way in oxcarts laden with children, bedding, clothing, furniture, and livestock.

Until a house could be built, Mrs. Shaw had to set up housekeeping in a large marquee tent they had brought with them. Despite the tremendous upheaval in her lifestyle, she innovated, improvised, nursed, fed, clothed, learned, and still had enough stamina and desire to entertain the scattering of neighbouring settlers, including pioneer homesteader John Glenn, who gave them some of his land. When Samuel Shaw completed his wool mill, his wife found herself in woollen retailing in addition to being the mother of one more child!

Ingenuity was the requisite of all pioneer mothers, as in the case of Jean Pinkham, wife of Calgary's first Anglican bishop. In the late 1890s the governor general, Lord Minto, due in Calgary for a church cornerstone ceremony, requested an "informal civic luncheon at the mounted police officer's mess." There was no such place. Mrs. Pinkham, suspecting the mounties' dining hall social graces to be somewhat less proper than those of her very busy husband, who was to host the affair, decided she should check on the arrangements.

Accordingly, she and one of her daughters quickly picked some garden flowers, gathered Pinkham linen, silver, and fine glassware, and headed for the fort's dining room. They found it contained only a table covered with a coarse cloth, decorated with an edging of parsley, the force's government-issue cutlery and glasses, bottles of pickles, plates of soda crackers, and a swarm of black flies!

Mrs. Pinkham and the girl cleared the table, resetting it with a linen cloth, glasses of nasturtiums, their own elegant silver and crystal, and added a generous scattering of sticky flypaper. Luckily, the policemen's waiter removed the flypaper before serving the wild duck by reaching over the guests' shoulders, including those of Lord Minto and his entourage.

Mrs. Pinkham's social skills were successful over the years because, in addition to mothering her six children and spearheading many church and community activities, she was the persuasive founder and first president of the Women's Aid Hospital Society whose leadership resulted in Calgary's first general hospital.

Elizabeth, wife of Methodist missionary Rev. John McDougall, had been brought up in orchard country of Grey County, Ontario. Besides raising six children in the wilderness, she often travelled

Over-reliance on Calgary's fickle climate and brief summer brought hardships they had never anticipated upon the shoulders of pioneer housekeepers. Many chores, such as the weekly washing, had to be done outdoors because the original settler's cabin was a one-room affair with little space for work activities, let alone leisure. Water hauled in buckets from nearby creeks or a well had to provide yeoman service for a busy family.
Courtesy Glenbow-Alberta Institute / NA–2041–1

beside her husband on hazardous journeys through the West long before civilization touched its far corners. Elizabeth McDougall recalled her husband once returning from Fort Benton country in Montana with a box of six apples, fruit she had not seen since her childhood days in Ontario. Only a pair of apples had survived the long, hot journey. "I put them on a shelf and looked at them for two days before I ate one," she said.

Another kind of unexpected treat was treasured by Alice Maud Douglas, wife of a railway builder who was tracklaying towards Calgary. She was the mother of three children and the family had been railway gypsies, living in a small cabin erected on a railway flatcar. For months they moved slowly west with the construction without Mrs. Douglas seeing another white woman.

Then, towards the end of 1883, Howard Douglas took charge of the big, new railway supply depot at Calgary. At last Alice Maud was able to move into a tiny house without wheels under it! A few months later she was reunited with a treasure, her pump organ that had arrived safely from the east by rail. She and her husband were accomplished singers. Soon she was playing the organ at the little Methodist church, he was singing in the choir, and there was music once again in the Douglas home.

My own mother, who came here as the bewildered fiancée of the man who had preceded her to the "wild west" by a few years, ultimately faced the perils of raising children. Somehow she inherited those mysteriously acquired "mother things" with which your own mother must have bombarded you and your siblings, regardless of nationality or generation. See if you recognize them:

"Children should be seen and not heard."

"Don't you dare stick out your tongue at me! The wind will change and you'll stay like that!"

"Just remember, I have eyes in the back of my head!"

"If 'ifs' and 'ands' were pots and pans, there'd be no work for tinkers."

"Curiosity killed the cat," to which we cheekily retorted when we had learned it, "But satisfaction brought it back."

Memorable among my mother's sayings was her crisp reply to little children who were rude enough to ask her age. "I'm as old as my tongue and a little older than my teeth!" That shut them up while they figured that one out.

Mother had one reply that was most useful when we were pushy or critical or impatient, "Fools and bairns should never see things half done!" And if we whined about having to complete certain hateful chores, "Why keep a dog and bark yourself?"

And what about the ageless "My Mother the Martyr" act, which, I believe, is God's free bonus gift to all mothers of all generations. Unfailingly performed with star-calibre skill, the script goes like this:

MOTHER: (*Looking hurt and woeful*) So you *are* going out, after all we've talked about?

YOU: (*Defiant. Smiling*) Yes, I *told* you I was, okay?

MOTHER: (*Sighing enormous sigh #1—created by God for all about-to-be abandoned mothers*) Oh yes, I'm all right. Just you go along and enjoy yourself. At least some of us can have fun. I'll manage alone, unprotected, in this big empty house (*huge sigh #2*) as long as I know you are not worrying about me. Being ignored is nothing new—to me!

Kids, for goodness' sake, GO! She is just being a mother who has lost another round. In a few years it will be you, using exactly the same wonderful Bette Davis histrionic skill.

Bless you, mothers, one and all. Your Oscar is in the mail!

Sandstone Was More Than a Whistle Stop

*I*n 1906 Calgary had an alderman named John Goodwin Watson who is remembered as Gravity Watson because of his tireless and successful efforts to establish a dependable gravity-activated water supply for the little city.

Watson's equally energetic contribution to this area was as a quarryman. Having arrived here in 1897 from his Ontario hometown of Clanwilliam, he established a quarry, a brickyard, and a railway flagstop named Sandstone on the south bank of the Bow River, west of the city. However, when he sold the business, Watson took the name with him and began quarrying in a cleft of the hills almost three miles northwest of Okotoks.

In 1906 the company was bought out by the Alberta Portland Cement Company and the bricks, instead of bearing the imprint of Watson, were stamped APCCO. Three years later, when the Canada Cement Company took over the operation, the bricks it produced carried its initials, C.C.CO.

By 1912 Sandstone was thriving. The cement company's hopes had been justified by its discovery of deposits of cementing clay. Four brickyards were going full tilt, and there was a railway station, store, and post office. That year, during the outdoor working season between March and November, eleven million bricks were produced. In 1913 the operation was enhanced by the firing of the brick kilns with natural gas from Bow Island. Although production was halted during World War I, its kilns were fired up again and brickmaking continued until 1924.

Not long ago I talked to Okotoks pioneer Winnie Hebson, daughter of Lizzie and husband Percy Pegler, who worked at the brick plant from 1912 to 1924. Percy was from Gloucestershire and got a job as a quarryman in the small valley settlement. When the quarry reached the end of its productive lifetime, Pegler bought the quarter-section townsite with a view to farming it, for it had good soil, good access, and an excellent water supply.

One of the provisions in the deal was that he supervise demolition of the plant, a transaction that paid off handsomely. He recovered carloads of stored bricks on the site, as well as those bricks used in the construction of the kilns and other plant buildings. Pegler and his crew found a ready market for them with the result that the railway spur line was busy loading and shipping tons of bricks for some time after the plant closure. Then he farmed the land until his retirement in 1951.

Sandstone now is marked by the mouldering vestiges of the brick plants and two brick houses, one of which was the plant superintendent's house and the other a post office. The house has been restored by the W.E. Thompson family, whose home it is now. The other brick house, also too awkward to move when the quarrying and brick-making ended, stands deserted, as does the 121-foot-tall brick chimney.

The little village also lives on in the vivid memory of Winnie Hebson, who has the rare distinction of being Sandstone born and bred. She was " . . . born at home in one of the little wooden houses and weighed only five pounds." She and other children played in the deserted brick house, using its plaster walls as blackboards. The

The tiny settlement of Sandstone, located about twenty-five miles southwest of Calgary, and now a ghostly neighbour of the town of Okotoks, was once a prolific local source of building material. Situated in a deep prairie cleft, it was the site of adjoining brick kilns, sandstone quarries, and a portland cement plant serviced by the CPR line between Calgary and Lethbridge. This is the only known photo of what the town looked like at the height of its productivity in 1912. Courtesy of Sandstone-born Winnie (Pegler) Hebson, Okotoks

youngsters from Sandstone rode their ponies or horse-drawn buggies westward for three-and-one-half miles to the little one-room Panima School, where Grades One to Nine were taught.

Winnie, on her horse named Lolly, rode with neighbour kids such as the Blades, Bereskys, Peachys, and Hursts, whose fathers were all brick-workers. She also recalls the raucous horn that warned the villagers that blasting was ready, and she described to me how the settlement was plagued by the influenza epidemic of 1918–19. Close contact with the people was off-limits so milk delivered from Cole's dairy farm was left out front and not brought to the door.

Normally, though, Sandstone was by no means isolated. The steep and narrow valley was the route of the Calgary-Macleod branch of the Canadian Pacific Railway. Four passenger trains each day and a greater number of freight trains, in addition to those loaded with Sandstone's brick and clay, thundered up and down the cleft in the hills.

Winnie Hebson told me that by flagging down a passenger train it was possible to go to Okotoks for a couple of hours' shopping for a fare of 25¢ return. Once a month her parents, Percy and Lizzie Pegler, would go to Okotoks by democrat along the valley trail behind Daisy, the cart-horse Percy used throughout the working week to pull his quarry dump-wagon.

In the heyday of its short production life Sandstone had, in a tight row along the railway track in the valley, the Canada Cement Brick Plant #11, the Sandstone Brick and Sewer Pipe Company, and the Burnvale Brick Company. Other firms, which vanished after probing briefly at the hillside deposits, shipped small quantities of pale yellow structural sandstone. Actually, beneath the fifteen-foot overburden there was more shale than sandstone and, for the most part, the brickmaking clay, as well as the stone and shale, lay in fairly thin layers.

The quite plentiful building-quality stone varied from undesirably hard to impractically soft. Some of it, due to mineral water stains, had a slightly blue tint that appealed to a very limited market even though it was harder and more workable than the popular Paskapoo sandstone.

Some of Sandstone's bricks were used for business blocks and homes in Calgary and Okotoks and in construction of the High River hospital. Its sandstone found its way into the walls of a school in Okotoks and a few buildings in Calgary. But both before and after its boom period early in the century, the Sandstone operations were borderline cases financially. It took only some labour unrest in 1923 to cause the absentee brick plant owners in Montreal to order the kiln fires extinguished for good.

The trains, even the diesel Dayliner in later years, just whistled through Sandstone but never stopped. Today they whistle at the Thompsons' and the slowly vanishing remnants of the community that, about three-quarters of a century ago, was Winnie Pegler Hebson's birthplace.

A Daring Young Man
in His Flying Machine

*I*n the southwestern sector of Calgary International Airport is its ancestor, McCall Field. For almost forty years of phenomenal local aviation growth it served as the hub of Calgary's air transportation.

In March 1939 Calgary's air terminal was moved beyond the edge of town to this new expanse of flatland on the far side of the Nose Creek Valley. Prior to that, the airport had been little more than a stubble field on the edge of the Renfrew district. At last, far from the constrictions of the city, McCall Field was hailed as one of Calgary's badges of progress, a recognition of its role in the air age.

As construction of the new terminal facility progressed there was some nervous haste about naming it and the field. The building that replaced the wartime hutments was readied for its official opening in 1956 when my one-time broadcasting teammate Don Mackay was mayor. Obviously there was a need for a more prestigious name than merely Calgary Airport. I pestered Don to bring before council the fact that among us was a flyer of such stature as to be worthy of exceptional recognition. I guess I was as pleased as anyone when I learned that Fred McCall, our across-the-street neighbour on Elbow Drive, was to be so honoured.

Fred R. McCall was born in Vernon, BC, and was an airman from the age of eighteen when he joined the Royal Flying Corps in Britain after having gone overseas in 1916 with Calgary's 175th Battalion. He gained a place of honour among Canada's finest aerial warriors during 1918. In that single year he was awarded the Distinguished Service Order, the Military Cross and Bar, and the Distinguished Flying Cross. He equalled fellow fighter pilot Billy Bishop's record of destroying five enemy aircraft in a single day and accounted for thirty-one "kills" in a four-month period. Before his combat duty was over, Fred McCall had accounted for thirty-seven enemy planes and two reconnaissance balloons.

Fred McCall's account of his first victory on 6 January 1918 was contained in a letter home:

> I was over enemy lines at about 9,000 feet when suddenly two Hun machines of the fastest and best German type came for me, and what a glorious battle we had among the clouds, with gunners and infantry watching their respective representative going for each other.
>
> The fight lasted about 15 minutes and oh, what a warm time it was! But God seemed to protect me from the 300 bullets the Huns fired. And after putting about 150 in one, his engine stopped and down he went. He waved goodbye as he went down and I waved back at him so I suppose there were no hard feelings. I saw him crash into the wire in front of the trenches. He may not have been killed but his machine was in an awful mess after striking the ground. When the other Hun saw his pal go down he didn't take long to clear off to the horizon I can tell you. When I landed I found I had six holes in my machine and my wireless had been cut off.

Those days of gentlemanly combat over, Fred McCall returned home but the gravity-bound life of a civilian was not full enough to calm the appetite of the restless spirit. Within a year of resuming life in Calgary he was the owner of two biplanes flying the "A

Class" prairie fairs in western Canada. He used to stage two hair-raising stunt performances a day, filling the rest of the time taking people for daylight flights.

It was on one such flip over the fairgrounds during the Calgary Exhibition and Stampede in 1919 that his engine failed shortly after take-off from centre field in front of the grandstand. Rather than risk a crash on the track, McCall coolly pancaked the plane on the top of the merry-go-round. He and the two sons of exhibition manager Ernie Richardson, thirteen-year-old Herbert and Ronald, eleven, were helped to the ground unhurt. Without delay McCall tried

raising money for a new aircraft by selling pieces of the wrecked machine to sightseers on the exhibition grounds for 25¢ a fragment!

Fred McCall earned Canadian Commercial Pilot's licence #5 in 1921 although he preferred the irresistible thrill of stunting. He staged air-ground races with famous car speedsters Barney Oldfield and Bill Endicott, and at an early Calgary air show he frightened and thrilled us all with a stunt I will always remember.

I had pedalled my bike across town to watch the show and stood with a crowd on the edge of the old airfield at Renfrew. McCall took off in a burst of stubble and dust, heading for the Nose

Creek Valley at the far end of the field. He was barely off the ground when his plane tumbled over the edge obviously to crash either on the hillside out of sight or down on the railway tracks. A fire engine thundered off to the rescue but at the rim of the hill the crew tumbled out and stood there clearly bewildered.

Suddenly, back at the side of the hangar, we clutched one another and ducked, for McCall roared out of the north, swooped over the hangar roof and clipped the windsock as he dropped to a landing.

To McCall it was a huge joke, the way he had power-dived off the lip of the valley, turned left, out of our view, and raced up the valley above the tracks until he made his "attack" on the airfield, bearing down upon us as we had our eyes glued on the "disaster scene" far out across the field!

In his more sombre moments Fred McCall pioneered mountain flying in a postwar Jennie, flying along the passes between Golden, Fernie, Banff, and Calgary. By 1928 he had his own airfield in the Bow Valley, west of the city, that he named McCall Field and from which he flew sightseers from eight o'clock in the morning until dusk.

That year he was hired by brewer Emil Sick to fly the largest aeroplane yet seen in southern Alberta, a Stinson Detroiter, from the factory to the foothills city. Powered by a 250-horsepower radial engine, it had a cruising speed of one hundred miles per hour, and a cargo capacity of 2,250 pounds or five passengers. It was to be the flagship of Great Western Airways and aboard with pilot McCall on that maiden flight were co-pilot Jack E. Palmer, the airline's president Emil Sick, and newspaperman Dan Campbell.

This plane, that seemed so enormous, caused quite a flurry following its flight from Detroit via Minneapolis, Fargo, and Regina, with a brief forced landing at Walsh. The machine was put to work on charter passenger and freight assignments with such financial success that soon McCall and Sick had built Great Western Airways' fleet to six aircraft of various types with much of the flying being done by McCall and Palmer.

One of Great Western's charters was the first airlift ever attempted of nitroglycerin. One hundred quarts in rubber-cushioned cans along with a box of dynamite, a most lethal load, made the journey safely with Fred McCall at the controls. The Shelby, Montana, to Calgary venture brought forth this comment from *The Calgary Herald* newsman standing near me as I, a bloodthirsty teenager, watched and waited for the big bang: "Sensing the danger, an air of expectancy hung over the landing field where about fifty spectators and flying men had gathered. Captain Fred R. McCall, manager of Great Western Airways, was at the controls. He bumped twice when the plane hit the ground and a sigh of relief went up when nothing out of the ordinary happened."

At the age of forty-four Fred McCall again donned an air force uniform, for another war had broken out. Too old for combat flying this time, he became an officer, commanding training squadrons at the Royal Canadian Air Force #1 Initial Training School in Toronto.

When he died in 1949 Fred McCall left a legacy of valour, achievement, legend, and service. He was one of the founders of Canada's system of civilian flying clubs and the first president of the Calgary Flying Club. He played hard and he worked hard and when his head was in the clouds so was his heart, his skill, and his daring, for he was a leather-helmeted aviator of the old school. He left us a flying son, too, Major Fred R. McCall, and a corner of Calgary that will always be remembered as McCall Field.

Soothing Soaks—
Satisfaction Guaranteed

Last night was bath night. Preparations began around Saturday supper time, with armloads of firewood restocking the woodbox beside the kitchen stove. The water reservoir, which was part of the stove adjoining the firebox, was refilled too.

That evening supper dishes were washed in a minimum of water heated in the biggest stove-top kettle that, refilled, was put back to work heating bath water. Some kitchens had a stubby iron water pump, with a short curvy handle, at the far end of the kitchen counter top. Otherwise water had to be fetched from the tall spindly one out in the back yard.

While the women of the family garnered towels, especially the biggest that served as a bath mat, the large tin bathtub (the shape of the Saddledome always reminds me of it) was brought into the kitchen from its hook out in the back porch, where it hung during the rest of the week.

As darkness fell on another Saturday, and with kettles refilled and steaming atop the hot fire in the kitchen stove, the ritual of bath night began. From the youngest of the family, working up to the eldest member of the clan, in a long-standing ritual order, everyone took a bath in the warm kitchen.

The water rarely was deep but usually it was hot and, the more often it was shared, the soapier it got even though hot water was added from time to time. When the youngsters' baths were completed, usually the much-used water was bailed by the pailful and hurled out into the night beyond the back door. Then the freshly filled tub was used in turn by the grownups. They were afforded the pleasure of dousing themselves with clean, hot rinse-water, which they poured over themselves from a long-handled metal dipper as a final gesture of the weekly Saturday night bath ritual.

The last time I saw one of those portable metal tubs was on what, today, is called Pump Hill. Joe and I were handymen in my father's construction firm. One job, on a particularly frosty autumn morning, was to "point" the corroded mortar on the brick chimney at the apex of a four-sided bungalow roof.

We hauled replacement bricks, trowels, strips of tin flashing, and a bucket of freshly mixed mortar up a ladder onto the crest of the roof. Joe warned me of the hazard of standing on the slippery areas of the roof where the morning sun had not yet burned off the frost. I, a brash and forgetful youth, scoffed at his timidity and, in a jiffy of carelessness, swooped in a flailing slalom down the roof, landing unhurt but shaken on the frosty grass at the back of the house.

Joe, tools in hand, stood by the chimney howling with laughter at my impromptu performance. Then without thinking he, too, stepped onto the "shady" side. I watched him windmill towards me, swoop down off the eaves and, while still airborne, pass me with a yell. I still recall the clang of his tool belt as he landed just beyond me in this old abandoned tin bathtub in the back yard.

Joe lay almost wedged upside down in it, recovering from the shock of his partly airborne slide. Later, when he was in a better mood, I teased him for his "Saturday night" flight from rooftop into bathtub.

Eighth Avenue East was the location of most, if not all, Turkish steam baths—well patronized by cowboys, who, on ranches, had to put up with a "community" towel, a tin wash basin, and homemade soap. Courtesy Glenbow-Alberta Institute/NA–2864–36429–#14–14A

A while ago I came across early evidence of some Calgarians' bathing habits. It was an advertisement from the late 1880s for the City Barber Shop and Bath House run by a Mr. Mark Cuzner. He let readers of the newspaper know that he offered the services of "Hot and Cold Baths at all hours. Best Work Done. Satisfaction Guaranteed." I wondered if unspoken, yet surely implied, "the best work" included having someone scrub your back?

Cuzner's discretion and moral integrity obviously were impeccable, for he advertised that his premises in the new Millward Building (next to the Star Bakery) on Stephen Avenue were reserved "Tuesdays and Fridays for Ladies."

Presumably gone forever from the Calgary scene are the public Turkish baths and steam baths of my youthful years that once upon a time catered with liniment and hot towels to our local businessmen, especially those who groaned across their thresholds seeking soothing and fast treatment of a hangover! I believe the last of these old-timers was the Calgary Turkish Steam Bath that puffed its last hot breath back in 1979 after seventy years' service on Third Street East at Seventh Avenue where the civic Administration Building now stands. I notice in today's telephone yellow pages only one public bath house is advertised, and it is for "Men Only."

One other thing struck me as my fingers walked through the latest phone book's yellow pages: perhaps we are more sanitary Calgarians than were our forefathers. For while we don't have bath houses, we do have within our pocketbooks' reach jetted and whirlpool tubs, ultra baths, Jacuzzis, hot tubs, and Roman baths for "residences of distinction."

The Compleat Calgarian

*F*or most of our city's lifetime every Calgarian—man, woman, and child—wore some sort of headgear. Whatever your age you were not completely dressed without a hat or cap.

No woman dared enter a church bareheaded, and if a funeral passed on the street men automatically doffed hats as a token of respect. In elevators and upon crossing a threshold to enter a house, hotel, theatre, and a good many stores, off came the cap or the hat.

Most men preferred a cloth peaked cap, the winter model having earflaps that, unused, were tucked up inside. Another popular adult male headpiece was a snap-brim Fedora hat with a wide ribbon band of the "Untouchables" type and era. The core of the youngster's cap peak was a piece of cardboard that you promptly bent and stomped on in the belief that the other kids at school wouldn't notice your brand new cap.

Women always wore hats in public. Mother had a hat-manufacturing cousin in Toronto who shipped her a gift of at least three elegant and ornate hats every six months or so. Huge brims, swirls of tulle, ribbons, osprey feathers, peacock plumes, and imitation fruit made them the envy of her peers at meetings of the Imperial Order Daughters of the Empire (IODE) and the Calgary Musical Club.

Because she could not afford a cross-country trip, Mother never knew if the hats were leftover samples of the past season, or breath-taking previews of fashions yet to come. It didn't matter, for they were the vanguard of Calgary's hat styles, they arrived postage-paid and, of course, they went right to Mother's head!

Locally the most famous hat of all, of course, is the cowboy hat, the centuries-old sombrero style of leather, wool, felt or, for summer wear, straw. Its high crown and broad brim made it a coveted possession of the cowman, who used it for everything from fanning a reluctant campfire to urging a balky horse, as a fly-swatter, drinking cup, pillow, and sunshade.

Cowboy hats in "ten-gallon" size or larger or smaller, and coloured fawn, brown, grey, or black, always appeared in profusion on the heads of rural visitors and competitors in the infield at the Calgary Stampede. The durability of felt made from coyote or beaver fur by Texas hatter John B. Stetson resulted in a burst of popularity and gave the name Stetson generic status.

A 1912 advertisement by "The Great Clothiers of the Great West," MacLeod Bros., featured Stetson hats in styles named "Columbia," "Dakota," and "Big Four," at Stampede sale prices ranging from $8.00 to $12.75. Stetson velour hats were very expensive for those days, $30.00. However, a cowboy's hat and his boots were his most valued possessions. So many considered an all-weather, long-lasting velour sombrero to be well worth a $30.00 outlay.

The hat was made with a large brim and taller crown, neither part having much shape. The cowboy's first concern when he had his new hat home on the ranch was to curl its brim and dent and crease its crown to make it an original. Funny, that's just what we did with our caps as nine-year-olds at school!

In the earliest days, sombrero dimensions were dictated by wind, brushland, and weather conditions on the range, although

In 1924 Guy Weadick hired Calgarian Jack Dillon as one of his "lieutenants" at the Stampede. Sharing the vital job of arena director gave Dillon plenty of opportunity to use his training as a livestock commission agent. Thanks to Calgarian Bill Herron, the white hat was becoming part of the Stampede's and, in fact, the city's "uniform." Jack Dillon's peers would have considered him undressed had he appeared without his trademark white hat. Courtesy Mary Dillon Collection

basically they all looked the same. Current movie stars such as Tom Mix, Harry Carey, Bill Hart, and Tex Ritter were seen with their special sombreros and soon local riders were showing their personal preferences in the same way.

Whatever the shape and dimensions, cowboys stuck to their superstitions that luck would spill out if the hat was laid down on its brim, and never were hats swapped. Neither did they choose white hats for the practical reason that they got grubby too fast— something that didn't matter a hoot with any hat that was off-white.

In Calgary, 1947 was a historic year in the life of the cowboy hat. Okotoks-born oilman William S. Herron and his family appeared in the Stampede Parade and took the "best dressed" prize. In Bill's words:

> We (the two boys, my wife, and I) had silver-mounted saddles and black and white horses. We wanted white hats to go with the black and white outfits. We went to Max Shumiatcher of Smithbilt Hats. He canvassed his suppliers and got samples but they were a real dirty white, just light color you might say.
>
> Finally he got word of stocks he could get from Russia. He had to buy a gross at a couple of dollars apiece but he didn't think they would sell.

The upshot was that Herron paid to have four samples shipped from the USSR. When all charges were paid they cost $24 each, whereas a Smithbilt cowboy hat was in the $9 price range.

The white hats worn by the Herron family in that 1947 parade were a sensation, and the timing was perfect. In 1948 the Calgary Stampeders football team made it to the Grey Cup in Toronto. The Herrons and others spearheaded the idea of a special train of Stampeder fans, a chuckwagon, western horses and riders, and a program of foothills city-type hoopla to set Toronto on its ear, whether Calgary won the Grey Cup or not.

Chosen as master of ceremonies for the journey and the Toronto show was a young Calgary radio announcer, Don Mackay. Fans were urged to wear distinctive Calgary white hats, so cardboard "cowboy hats" were turned out locally and taken along. Toronto entertainment details were worked out on the train trip east with the additional help of celebrants such as Clifton Cross, Ed O'Connor, and Stu Adams, as well as a square dance team, and Jac Friedenberg's small dance band.

In Toronto the white hats wowed crowds, especially on the heads of the splendidly outfitted Herrons. It is said some were "liberated" right from the heads of Calgarians, and the cardboard versions, at $4, sold like hotcakes.

In 1950 Don Mackay, by that time a high-profile Calgarian whose symbol had become the white hat, was elected mayor and held the post until 1959. During his tenure, which was typified by many civic achievements, the "front and centre" mayor's white cowboy hat was seen and copied throughout the city. The presentation of a white hat became the highlight of a civic welcome to the city, and was worn with panache by VIPs including the Duke of Edinburgh, who received his in 1951.

On 3 October 1983 the City of Calgary chose its official flag. In colours of red and white, the design incorporates the white Stetson flowing in unison with the letter C, symbolizing harmony between the City of Calgary and the hospitality and zesty spirit of her people.

The Whistle Told Us the Time

When this century was very new, the Canadian Pacific Railway decided to undertake the enormous task of creating a network of irrigation canals, fed by Bow River waters, to nourish crops that it felt could be grown by new farmer-settlers in the water-poor Palliser Triangle. In the course of the ensuing decade the railway, with admirable foresight, realigned its mainline tracks on the eastern outskirts of Calgary to skirt the feeder canal, avoiding construction of extra bridges, and providing a large stretch of dead level prehistoric riverbed land for its own future company expansion.

Crucial to its plans were the anticipated rapid growth of rail networks across the Prairies, the promise of heavy transmountain traffic, the ideal location within the boundaries of the still small city of Calgary, the prospective availability of urban transit and of city-serviced worker housing, and the presence of an already established labour force. So, despite a strong pitch from the city of Medicine Hat, the CPR selected Calgary as the site of its planned new shops.

Preparation of the 156-acre site and erecting twelve buildings, constructing a 151,000-gallon water tank atop a sixty-nine-foot steel tower, laying twenty-two miles of track, and providing storage for 8 million board feet of lumber was a huge task for nearly fifteen hundred men and their teams of horses and mules. The complex also was to include a foundry, mess hall, apprentice classroom, offices, food services, paint and carpentry shops, a volunteer fire department, doctors' offices, and a big greenhouse to produce plants and shrubs to enhance railway gardens throughout the Prairies.

The whole job was completed in eleven-and-one-half months and the plant was opened in mid-March 1913. Immediately it was given a very loud voice, audible in the farthest corners of the city. A steam whistle, blown with the clockwork precision of "railroad time," it brazenly announced when it was time to begin work, to stop for lunch, to return to work, and to pack it up for the day. For sixty years, it blew four times daily, so accurately that generations of Calgarians set their clocks and watches by the Ogden Whistle. Near the plant there grew a diversified suburb of Ogden, light-heartedly referred to as "The Capital of Calgary." Land speculators poured into the area to flog the merits of a host of potential residential areas. Adjoining Ogden on the south was Cepeear, which, today, would border Glenmore Trail and Twenty-fourth Street SE, and next to it was Maharg. On the west were Millican Estate, bearing the name of pioneer rancher W.J. Millican, and Lynwood Ridge.

Real estate firms extolled the inevitable magnetism of the railway's undertaking as a workers' paradise, for the city limits had recently been extended to Eighty-second Avenue and the shops were only four-and-one-half miles from the centre of Calgary. Soon an imaginative naming spree labelled Ogden's northerly neighbours as Cossar, Valleyfield, and Harvetta Heights. To the east the shops were edged with Maryland, Hyde Park, Springwell Park, and Prospect Place.

Retail businesses soon moved onto the Ogden scene. Even before the shops were officially opened, the neighbourhood shopping area contained a branch of each of the Bank of Montreal;

Western Canada's largest heavy industry, the CPR Ogden Shops, opened in 1913 on the southeast edge of Calgary. The shops built and repaired locomotives and every type of the company's rolling stock. For years it was Calgary's largest employer. During World War I, much of the plant's capacity was diverted to the manufacture of naval guns and other heavy armament items. This interior view shows engines being shopped inside one of the locomotive foundries at Ogden. **Courtesy Glenbow-Alberta Institute/NA–4658–17**

Findlay Drug Company Ltd.; D.E. Black, Jeweller; and Crown Lumber Company. All were branches of midtown Calgary establishments. The railway built a three-storey red brick Ogden Hotel at the entrance to the plant for use by visiting CPR VIPs, and, in addition, there were two other Ogden hotels, as it was rumoured that a workforce of five thousand men soon would be employed in the sprawling shops.

It was all a highly optimistic far cry from the days when a pair of ranchers named Loaks and Weil ran horses on the property, and pioneers J.C. Wilson, William McIntyre, Millican, and Cossar had their spreads along the east bank of the Bow downstream from Calgary.

Named after CPR vice-president of finance and accounting, I.G. Ogden, the newly opened shops immediately took on building and repairing rolling stock in step with the railway's Montreal Angus and Winnipeg Weston heavy-duty plants. At Ogden more than half a dozen overhead rolling cranes with capacities of 120, 20, and 10 tons moved entire locomotives and other tracked units along assembly lines. One innovative Ogden-designed and -built machine rotated an entire freight or passenger car for complete access during acetylene welding repairs or construction.

Ogden land fever soon modified, in part because scores of the employees took advantage of commuter train service set up by the railway. It enabled many workers to retain their Calgary homes. Sunnyside was one of the districts where many lived and, when the Calgary Municipal Railway laid its streetcar tracks to Ogden, that community became the destination of many double-header trams operating on a schedule arranged to fit working hours at Ogden.

The Ogden run was immensely popular. Streetcars and their motorless trailers parked all day on special sidings near the plant gates handling the jam-packed horde of riders at either end of the working shift. Old-timer Bill Brisdon recalls how the untended and awaiting empty cars were visited. "In the summertime, the kids of Ogden would fish for tickets out of the fare box, by using a grasshopper on a string." Another recollection was of a streetcar freight run that handled cans of milk from local farms and delivered merchandise to Ogden's retail stores.

To meet big and urgent demands of World War II, part of the plant had to be scrubbed and retooled for the manufacture of munitions and armament. At a time when twenty-five hundred men were working at Ogden, nineteen hundred of them on munitions, Ogden Shops manufactured 1,001 twelve-pounder naval guns and mountings, twice that number of six-pounder naval gun barrels, in addition to hundreds of Bofors gun mountings and quantities of four-inch gun sights and mountings.

Back in civilian life Ogden Shops, for many years Calgary's leading employer, went back to full-capacity railway work, adjusting with the times, always handling the increasingly heavy locomotives and rolling stock from Winnipeg west in its role as the Mountain Shop.

It outshopped its last steam locomotive No. 5212, a 2-8-2 Mikado freight hauler, in June 1957, as diesel-electric locomotives began to dominate the motive-power scene. But the Ogden Shops, in a continuing modernized role as rebuilder, repairer, repainter, and track equipment maintainer, still sustains a strong industrial heartbeat in the Ogden community that now, more than ever before, is part of our Calgary.

What a Choice—The Pain or the Cure

*E*ither modern illnesses are more complicated than they used to be or, if we are not sick, we seem determined to invent new ones. Help for what, in memory, were the simpler ailments of yesterday, came from the neighbourhood druggist, whose place of business was known as a plain, unadorned drugstore.

Back then, the word "drug" almost invariably meant a panacea, not a mind bender. Most of those drugstores stocked a small and predictable assortment of goods that somehow seemed a logical extension of the pharmacy itself: over-the-counter remedies, Kodak cameras and film, Lowney's and Moir's boxed chocolates, post cards, and toiletries.

Calgary's first druggist appears to have been Samuel Trott, who was in business here in 1883. Other names that pop up in memories of my own young days are McGill, Findlay, Higginbotham, Maclean, Crooks, Penley, Mahood, and MacMillan.

Once in a while someone phones to say, "You know, I used to ride my bike winter and summer for a nickel a trip for so-and-so's drugstore." Together we remember druggists like Black in Hillhurst; Holmes in Victoria Park; Friedman in Sunalta; McDermid in town and out at Sarcee Village; and Dunford, Temple-Duff, and Farrow in the downtown core.

Although eastern drug company salesmen cruised the nation showing doctors the latest pharmaceuticals, the big local wholesaler was the National Drug and Chemical Company of Canada Ltd., called "the National" in spite of the firm trying to use its rather absurd abbreviation of "NaDruCo." For years, until replaced by the Bentall Building, its big red brick warehouse stood on Seventh Avenue directly behind Eaton's store.

If the ailments of yesterday were simple, so were the treatments (not necessarily cures!) I was always morbidly fascinated by the pink medicated fluffy cotton pad that Mother applied to treat a chest cold. It was called Thermogene and, to boost its poulticing capabilities, she would sprinkle it with a few drops of her precious #4711 cologne. That would stoke its fire until your hide was grilled!

Another poultice treatment was Antiphlogistine, which became known as Thermofuge—pasty stuff folded into cotton sheeting and safety-pinned into your pyjama top. A hot soap and bread poultice was applied to suck at a boil on your neck or a splinter under your thumbnail. There was no escape from that kind of heat while it allegedly lured the "poison" out of your inflamed skin.

A more exotic infection-fighter, a bichloride of mercury tablet dissolved in warm water into which you dipped your sore pinkie, was part of the druggist/mother conspiracy. The fact was, the

Opposite: *McGill's drugstore was one of the very popular pharmacies in southwest Calgary. Billy McGill was everyone's favourite, making himself and his chemist's skills and services available to anyone needing medication, day or night. His prompt and reliable home delivery service by lads on bicycles in any weather for what might seem the most trifling prescription or health care item was almost legendary. This photo of the interior of the McGill drugstore shows William McGill behind the tobacco counter,* (centre). *Note the ice-cream chairs and tables.*
Courtesy Glenbow-Alberta Institute/NA–4026–3

druggist's pharmacy shelves were laden with some pretty horrible ingredients and concoctions, his entire arsenal being locked in a conspiracy with the weird treatments your mother inherited from her mother.

What he didn't produce, she did. I am thinking of an improvised red flannel collar, or a well-worn and unwashed man's woollen sock, pinned around your young scrawny neck for a sore throat. A druggist's remedy was the second line of Mother's artillery. She would insist that you sniffle salty water up your nose, which did little more than start a headache from having drowned your sinuses.

The druggist had a chest remedy, Camphorated Oil, a mix of camphor and olive oil. He had Castor Oil that put you off the taste of oranges for years. Friar's Balsam was a sore throat horror, either a few drops swallowed on a lump of sugar or inhaled, as you sat with your head swathed in a towel snuffling the medicated steam from the kettle.

Mother had one sore throat cure inherited from some bizarre relative. She would firmly tie a small glob of fatty bacon on a linen thread. You swallowed the bacon and she would withdraw it by the thread for a second and third swallow! It was very effective. You see, it was such an off-the-wall performance that never again were you stupid enough to report a sore throat.

For colds and fever one prescription was quinine in white capsules swallowed with water—fast. Actually, for incessantly fretting babies at teething time, the druggist sold parents Paregoric, a soother containing morphine! He recommended treating rheumatism with his prescription of sodium salicylate and flavouring in a simple syrup. In fact, one long-time druggist admitted the sugar and water mixture was a standard carrier for most of the powders that emerged from his mortar and pestle department.

Apparently there were prescriptions a druggist could knock off in a wink, others were miserable to compound. One unpopular one, prescribed by a doctor and prepared by a druggist, was a treatment for indigestion: forty grains of powdered charcoal liquified in essence of pepsin. It was one of those messy concoctions that made old-time druggists welcome many prepackaged and prebottled patent medicines that began filling their shelves.

Do you remember some of them? Fowler's Extract of Wild Strawberry, Templeton's TRC (Templeton was a Calgarian), Lydia E. Pinkham's Vegetable Compound, Williams' Pink Pills for Pale People, the laxative cascara sagrada marketed as Casagra, Scott's Emulsion, iron-rich Parrish's Food that you gulped lest it stained your teeth, Kepler's Cod Liver Oil and Malt, and Wampole's Cod Liver Extract. Often, in those days, feeling poorly was much preferable to taking the so-called cure.

Just before cosmetics began tapping the mother lode of feminine vanity, the druggist recommended witch hazel as a facial astringent, and kohl, a powder, for eye shadow. Maybe, in many instances, only the packaging has become exotic. Whatever has changed, the basic ailments continue to plague us. Which reminds me of the hypochondriac's tombstone that read: "See, I *told* you I was sick!"

À Calgary Nous Parlons Français

Roman Catholic missionaries were already here when, in the summer of 1875, F Troop of the mounted police reached the meeting place of the Bow and Elbow rivers. There they saw the lone tent of Father Constantine Scollen out on the empty prairie of the valley bowl that would become the site of their fort and, in time, the city of Calgary.

In 1872 the Catholic churchmen had built a small log mission higher up the Elbow. Three years later, spurred by the commencement of construction of Fort Calgary, the mission building was stripped by Father Doucet and Father Scollen and floated downstream to a low knoll where it was relocated immediately south of today's Holy Cross Hospital.

When at first it was believed the railway would establish its townsite east of the Elbow, a Catholic St. Patrick's church was built there. But with the railway's decision to create a town west of the river, Father Lacombe and his colleagues had the church moved to where it became the first of several successive St. Mary's houses of worship.

Another busy Oblate missionary in this part of the West was Father Albert Lacombe, who was particularly adept at winning the trust and cooperation of the Indians. His many activities, all dedicated to church works and the projection of the faith he shared, were, in today's terms, high profile.

In 1885 the Northwest Territories Council empowered the lieutenant governor to create a board of education composed of two groups—six non-Catholics and six Catholics—each being placed in charge of schools in its section. To honour Father Lacombe one element in this area was named the Lacombe Roman Catholic Separate School District #1.

That soon had to be changed, not because it was a mouthful, but because financial supporters in central Canada were confused as to the geographical destinations of their contributions. So the title was changed from Lacombe to Calgary. The door was now open for the official establishment of a nondenominational boarding school by the Roman Catholic sisters, the Faithful Companions of Jesus .

Four nuns, frontier teachers near Batoche, were urged by Bishop Vital Grandin to escape the perils of the Riel Rebellion and move to Calgary, and that they did with considerable vigour and success, under the guidance of Rev. Mother Mary Greene. In Calgary Father Lacombe offered the nuns his rectory as a Sacred Heart Convent in which they could establish St. Mary's School.

Although Father Lacombe was moving about the area constantly, his home base was a small farmstead next to the site of the future St. Mary's Parish Hall. A short distance to the west was a small church with an absurdly large tower housing an eight hundred-pound bell nicknamed the "Alberta Josephine." With the construction of a convent and school in 1886, the knot of church buildings occupied one corner of the land adjoining the Elbow River south of Calgary's townsite.

Realizing "squatter's rights" were not enough, Father Lacombe, impatient to avoid the bureaucracy of obtaining permission from his superior, Vicar-General Father Hippolyte Leduc, set off for Ottawa. There, by threatening to camp outside the office of the minister of the interior if necessary, he promptly received homestead title to more than the occupied land, two quarter-sections, in the names of Lacombe and Leduc.

In 1886 Magistrate Charles B. Rouleau, a member of the Territories' board of education, moved to Calgary. His brother Hector, newly appointed to the position of chief surgeon to the mounted police, moved here the same year, and they both became residents of the same neighbourhood.

In 1891 the size of the Roman Catholic settlement was augmented by the opening of the Holy Cross Hospital, a small two-storey, four-patient refuge just to the west of the cathedral site in the parish of St. Mary's. The area, yet to be annexed by Calgary, was known as Rouleauville. There were no streets or lights between the CPR station and Nineteenth Avenue. Those four original Montreal-trained Grey Nuns, facing the task of establishing the hospital, walked with their baggage in the perishing cold of that 30 January night.

The unfinished building must have been a most discouraging destination at the end of that dark, frigid walk. The quartet is said to have had total assets of $209.74 and about $150 worth of belongings. But, like the school-teaching nuns before them, they gave everything they had by way of courage and effort to successfully accomplish their assignments.

It was not until 1907 that Rouleauville was annexed to Calgary. The streets and avenues that had borne such names as St. Joseph, St. Mary, Oblate, Lacombe, and Doucet, were allocated numbers in keeping with the city's 1904 system of numbering the existing grids. Not only did the area lose much of its French-Canadian character, it did not attract nearly as many French-speaking Canadians as had been anticipated. More and more settlers from Ontario, Britain, and the United States settled there.

The Anglicization of it was typified, as I clearly recall, by the fact that we all knew a Mission hardware store as "Dess-pins," although the family name was Des Pins and they spelled it that way. Notre Dame Road was assigned the dull title of Seventeenth Avenue, and Broadway, with allegiance to neither faction, became Fourth Street West. What might have become Calgary's French Quarter, especially after the demise of the Rouleau brothers, paid pallid tribute to its settlers by becoming the Mission District long after the mission had vanished.

In his advanced years, Father Lacombe concentrated his efforts upon creating one of his life's dreams, a haven for the aged and orphaned. His giant brick Lacombe Home still stands on the hilltop in northeast Midnapore within sight of today's No. 2 Highway. That first hospice, where he spent his final years until his death in December 1916, has outlived its usefulness. Its hilltop companions are a modern Father Lacombe Nursing Home for the elderly, and the Inter-Faith Lacombe Centre.

In 1933 five Basilian Fathers came to Calgary to join the administration and teaching staffs of St. Mary's School. The school enrolment was divided in 1907, and the boys' school first held classes in the original parish hall. At St. Mary's the talented and revered Father Jim Whelihan coached many local athletes. Of him it was said once, "He not only makes athletes, he makes gentlemen."

St. Mary's is the survivor of Calgary's midtown schools. Beginning as a boarding school, it was the first Separate School in Alberta. The present building stands within 110 yards of the first Sacred Heart Convent where it all began. More than that, it is within a stone's throw of the tent the mounted police spotted from the high edge of the riverbank in 1875.

On the southern edge of Calgary the Oblate Fathers, Sisters of the Faithful Companions of Jesus (usually known as the Grey Nuns), along with missionary Father Lacombe and other Roman Catholic churchmen, established a French-speaking enclave. Before becoming known as the Mission District of Calgary, it was called Rouleauville, after its most distinguished resident, Justice Charles B. Rouleau, stipendiary magistrate of the Northwest Territories. This 1887 photo of the area looks north to the town of Calgary, beyond Rouleauville, along what became Fourth Street, past the Elbow River. Courtesy Glenbow-Alberta Institute /NA–431–4

The Long Western Life of Lillian Train

*T*he days of our years are threescore years and ten; and if by reason of strength they be fourscore years, yet is their strength labour and sorrow." So says the psalm.

An outstanding exception was Margaret Lillian Leigh Moss Stinson Train, a sprightly little woman whose physical dimensions were minor compared to her ample name, and whose memory was truly remarkable. Lillian arrived at the small Holy Cross Hospital in 1894, the second of three daughters and one son born to Elizabeth and Joseph Moss.

Joseph Higginbotham Saxon Moss was a driver on the ox-train route between Fort Benton and Fort Calgary in the late 1870s and early 1880s. He became a part-time wagoner in 1882 and established, on the wagon route at Pine Creek, a homestead that he named the Edgehill Ranche.

In June 1888 Joseph Moss married Elizabeth Shortt in the recently erected Knox Presbyterian Church on McTavish and McIntyre (Centre Street and Seventh Avenue) in Calgary.

The Moss children became skilled riders as Edgehill Ranche won recognition for its driving and trotting horses and polo ponies. In 1901 Joseph sold Edgehill and moved east to a bigger spread on Arrowwood Creek directly east of Okotoks, a dot on the map adjoining the Blackfoot Indian Reserve. Today it is the hamlet known as Mossleigh, being a reverse combination of two of the family names Lillian inherited from her antecedents.

It took them six rain-drenched days to make the move with the family belongings piled aboard a couple of hay racks while herding their horses and seventy head of cattle. Just a ploughed fireguard separated their new spread from the Indians' land, and soon they established a splendid repartee with the Blackfoot ranchers along their north boundary.

The winter of 1906–07 took a terrible toll of livestock on the windblown prairie. Lillian recalled how her father rounded up some Indians to help him search his land once the snow began to melt. The rancher's only financial salvation was to reclaim the frozen carcasses.

Joseph Moss struck a bargain that he would have the hides, and the Indians could have the meat. One day Lillian's mother raised a great fuss when the group returned to the ranch with their haul. She loudly claimed the deal had become very unfair. The Indians, she stormed, were getting far too much meat. The leader of the Indian group, Joe Fatback, listened to the tirade as long as he could, then turned to Joseph and said, "Your squaw, she too much bleh bleh bleh!"

One memorable part of Lillian's life on that Long Valley Ranche was the lack of schools. Elizabeth Moss was a stickler for education so the family acquired a governess, apparently an "iron maiden," from Ontario, whose unbending reign was respected with reluctance by the Moss girls. She was succeeded by an English tutor with the rather unlikely name of Elijah Cobham. Both Moss parents had died by 1914, so Lillian came to Calgary to live with cousins while she successfully completed a business course at Mount Royal College.

Margaret Lillian Leigh spent the early years of her long life on a horse and became a skilled rider whose "born to the saddle" skill was admired by all the ranch, farm, and trick competition riders she met. Daisy Parsons, Lillian's friend and a fellow fancy rider who typified many of Lillian's accomplishments, is pictured here at the 1919 Calgary Stampede. Courtesy Glenbow-Alberta Institute/NA–558–2

In those days the Pacific Cold Storage Company of Tacoma owned several ranches, a packing house, and retail meat markets in Rosebud, Hussar, Brooks, Bassano, and their headquarters town of Gleichen. In that town, for over five years, Lillian was secretary to the firm's Canadian manager, Chris Bartsch, who, in addition to his company duties, was a keen organizer of local rodeos.

One day, at the Gleichen Stampede, it happened that "a queen bee of barrel racers" who hailed from Great Falls had no competitor. Nobody was eager to give her the prize by default. Bartsch, knowing his young steno was an accomplished rider, made Lillian leave her desk, still dressed in hobble skirt and blouse, to give the American girl some opposition. Borrowing Smoky, a Clem Gardner horse experienced in barrel racing, Lillian won the contest hands down, much to the chagrin of the visitor and the delight of the local crowd.

In 1918 Lillian became the wife of Isaac Edward Stinson from North Dakota. Together they built a solid retail business in Carseland. After twenty-five years and Ed's untimely death, the "unsinkable" Lillian turned her business experience to good use by moving to Calgary and chopping her official age from fifty to forty-four! She worked for Prudden's china shop on Eighth Avenue West and, when the firm changed hands, became manager of a new North Hill Shopping Centre company store from 1959 until her retirement in 1965.

That was the year she married farmer Angus Train of Claresholm. Lillian chuckled, "I was a rancher who had to learn to be a farmer!" She remembered Angus and his cronies talking about how good the summer fallow was coming along, something foreign to a rancher. They certainly teased her when she innocently asked, "What does this summer fallow crop look like when it's ready for market?"

Lillian recalled trying to untangle flax, a new experience for her, working in the high winds of Claresholm country out in front of the combine. "Suddenly the windrows of flax took off like coyotes, out to the horizon."

Even at age ninety-four, Lillian Train was a scrapbook-aholic. She showed me a one-hundred-year-old wedding photo of her mother and father, with a most visible bandage on the groom's left hand. Joseph Moss was left-handed and always drove with a loaded shotgun propped against the front of the buggy. Just before his wedding day he picked it up by the barrel to prod the horses into a trot. The gun went off. Joseph, with a badly mangled wrist, ripped open a bag of flour in the back of the buggy and plunged his hand deep into the flour to staunch the blood until he reached a doctor. Upon learning of this his fiancée Elizabeth vowed he needed someone right away to take care of him.

One more anecdote worth retelling: Senator Pat Burns was a close family friend. One day the short stocky visitor to Edgehill Ranche dandled dark-eyed, curly-haired Josephine and blue-eyed, straight-haired Lillian on his lap. Fondly gazing at one, his comment was "Beautiful Josie." "Then," recalled Lillian, "looking at me he was a bit stumped until, and from then on, he called me 'Elegant Lil.'" And that, indeed, she was until her final days at age ninety-five.

Calgary's Noisiest and Smelliest Acres

*T*he Calgary Public Livestock Market is an institution nearly as old as our city yet firmly in tune with today's technology.

As long ago as 1886, the year of the first CPR through train to the Pacific Ocean, and Calgary's second birthday, the town council suggested some land should be set aside for a stockyard. The following year, feeling its oats, as it were, council offered the railway some of its town land on a two-year lease basis.

The railway went one better. Encouraged by the growing presence of Pat Burns's nearby abattoir and meat-packing facilities, it rented out (as a stockyard) twenty-four acres downwind from the little city. Today, although the railway now has its own huge real estate division, the tenant remains in place on that same parcel.

Back in 1903 the CPR, the only mass transporter of livestock, offered trackside service to cattlemen and soon several commission agents were headquartered in aptly named "Burnsland." For the cattle ranchers it was a fine set-up. They drove their herds up the Macleod Trail, or west through Hubalta, or eastward across the North Hill, down Fourth Street East (or Hay Hill because of the hayfeed spilled on the slope) and out to the stockyard. Until the late 1920s herds of four to five hundred cattle were trailed through the little city.

On sales days the commission agents would take their small percentage for handling the sales and the stockyard would take another fee as a yardage charge. Herders and cattle dealers congregated at the Stockyards Hotel to swap yarns over a beer, while the air outside vibrated to the lowing of penned cattle awaiting shipment in the railway's wooden-slatted, white-and-red cattle cars, or a quicker fate at the adjoining Burns plant. It is interesting that nearly every old-timer worked at Burns in his younger days.

The stockyard had a horse ring in back of the hotel, and handled thousands of head of horses, swine, and sheep, for Calgary was a terminal market—a transfer point of great importance. It had outstripped Fort Macleod, which, hitherto, had been the marketing centre for cattle on the hoof.

One day I got yarning at the stockyard with old-timers Len Friesen and Stan "Buck" Rothwell. At one point auctioneer Bruce Flewelling dropped in, as did the "youngster" of the group, Will Irvine, the livestock market's general manager. Len had begun working in the stockyard, a block from his home, carrying calves into the selling ring. Buck and Will had worked with shovels and buckets as muckers, the way just about every old-timer started, with a shovel or a water hose.

The conversation was peppered with reminiscences and names: commission agents such as Parslow and Denoon, who came on the scene in 1915; Adams, Wood, and Weiller in 1919; Paul and Macdonald; A.H. Mayland, Hammill, Starke; the Dvorkins, Sol, Hymie, and Tony; Bill Renard, George Winklaar, Charlie Kennedy, who was stockyard manager; auctioneers Earl Galvin and Harry Vold, Jim Raffin and his son Don, and Archie Boyse, as well as a host of others from the past and present.

We talked of the wooden T-bridge above the stockyard, with the Ogden streetcars rumbling across it. Then there was the motorist

The Calgary Public Livestock Market was its official title, but every citizen and rancher knew the twenty-four acre, white-fenced checkerboard, with its overhead walkways, as "the stockyards." At the time this photo was taken, early in the century, at least one trainload of live cattle left the city daily for Ontario markets and slaughterhouses. **Courtesy Glenbow-Alberta Institute/NA–2230–1**

who drove up the "leg of the T" and kept going through the white wooden railing, ending up in his wrecked car embedded in the unsavoury mud of a cow pen.

During World War I the Calgary Public Stockyard annually cleared around 100,000 cattle, 26,000 horses, 125,000 hogs, and 25,000 sheep. The veterans told me they have handled as many as 320,000 head a year between the mid-1950s and early 1970s. In World War II hogs were in great demand for export, with the Burns plant handling as many as 3,000 animals daily and the stockyard nearby putting through as many as 5,000 head of cattle on the hoof just on a Friday.

One of the tragic stories told by the old-timers recalled the Dirty Thirties. With no cattle feed in dust-blown Saskatchewan, the Calgary yard used to receive trainloads of starving beef cattle that marketed 1¢ and 2¢ per pound and, in each lot, five or six emaciated animals labelled "of no market value."

Through the years marketing was "policed" by federal government inspectors who ensured correctness in all shipping paperwork. Animals were held here for a seventy-two-hour quarantine period while being tested for every possible disease, and government brand inspectors constantly prowled the yards.

One major change was the departure of the Co-op, which sought to establish a state-of-the-art livestock facility near the airport. That ended disastrously. Then there was another upheaval, the introduction of cattleliner trucks in the mid-1950s, enabling farmers to truck their live beef directly to eastern or southern markets, by-passing the Calgary yards and the railway. That led to the end of most livestock commission firms and the establishment of the livestock auction mart concept. Next, along came electronics. Today across Canada twenty-four offices are in computer communication. That means livestock transactions, even in times of fickle auction market activities, are consummated in seconds between the barometer of the nation's fat cattle market—the Calgary Public Livestock Market—and its customers.

Many years ago at nine o'clock on a business morning the stockyard office building janitor would raise the flag above the rooftop, signalling the start of the day's business. Throughout each marketing day deals were completed by a handshake, and they tell me that tradition of trust is still dominant.

For years on each trading morning when the flag had gone up, buyers flipped coins to see who was first on the trading floor. As each load of cattle arrived, coins were matched again, and so it went until trading was over for the day. The old-timers could not remember any double-headed coins or shifty stuff, although many buyers cherished their "lucky" coins. If you won the toss and your initial bid was not good enough, you waited your chance to make a better offer.

Today, the computer readout has replaced the coin. Cattleliner trucks have replaced the twenty to thirty rail-car loads of live beef cattle that used to head out of here daily. Yet, in 1987, only 7,551 live head went to distant markets by truck. Now the demand is for dressed beef carcasses, nearly fifty thousand of them in 1987, for example, all marketed by computer from those same twenty-four leased acres where it all began.

Many Volleys Fired in Fun

*I*t appears that our settlement at the junction of the Bow and Elbow rivers was very young when settlers played the first game of tennis here. Elderly records date it in the early 1880s on a flat piece of barracks ground within Fort Calgary. A short time later, players paced out a court on what was to be named Prince's Island where tennis was played in the summer of 1884.

When townspeople discovered they could mark out a court, equip it with a net, tennis balls, and a couple of racquets for less than $15, several families began playing tennis alongside their homes. Among them was land developer Freddie Lowes, who played the game in attractive treed surroundings at Lowestoft, his home at the edge of the Elbow River at the north end of his new residential development of Elbow Park. Players with smaller residential property banded to form clubs.

A few years ago, one of those early groups celebrated its seventy-fifth anniversary. The very first group, according to our local doyen of sports historians, Bill McClennan, was formed in 1888. A year later it pitted its members' skills against those of the local mounted police tennis players on a court at the northwest corner of Seventh Avenue and Centre Street. Then, when the mounties improved their court at the fort by surfacing it with shale, they challenged the newly formed Calgary Lawn Tennis Club to a tournament in 1894.

Two blocks north of there tennis was played on a privately owned court alongside the row of little houses that today, faced by store-fronts, still stand on the east side of Centre Street in Chinatown between Fourth and Third avenues.

In 1905 the tournament-hungry Calgary Lawn Tennis Club moved from its base of operations, Centre Street property rented from William Roper Hull, to land bought from the CPR at the lower edge of Mount Royal. There, at Eighteenth Avenue and Ninth Street, two courts were steadily booked under the cooking hot summer sun on the bald, treeless prairie.

Tennis whites, of course, were mandatory clothing for players, including the women's voluminous ankle-length dresses, even in those days of heavy oval racquets and dirt, and cinder or prairie grass courts. The dusty players always retired to the wooden shelters that served as clubhouses and drank tea, this being a very social and somewhat snobbishly elegant sport.

The Calgary Tennis Club doubled its capacity to four shale courts on its Eighteenth Avenue property and that is where, in 1907, a provincial tournament was held on what were said to be the West's finest tennis courts. The Calgary club also hosted the provincial tournament in 1909, drawing a large gallery even though the Calgary Municipal Railway had not yet managed to lay track along Seventeenth Avenue, as had been hoped, in order to bring spectators to watch the contest.

Mr. Hull, one of our wealthier citizens, noted for his business acumen and philanthropy, was a great tennis booster. He and his wife, Emmeline Mary, sponsored many social gatherings of the tennis set, in particular the annual Tennis Winter Ball. They were host and hostess at that gala event held in the Hull Opera House on Centre Street. The Hull home's spacious lawn on Twelfth Avenue and Fifth Street West included a splendid grass court, scene of a

No matter how few settlers or how barren their surroundings, there was always a yearning among some immigrants from "the Old Country" for a game of tennis. These original courts, cleared of gopher holes and sage plants, and levelled from the prairie soil, became the sporting home of those immigrants whose luggage included a racquet and some tennis balls. They used whatever raw materials were available to fashion the chalked lines and nets needed for a game of tennis on the frontier. Courtesy Calgary Tennis Club, Larry Kennard photograph succession of tennis-and-tea gatherings each summer. In fact, it was a matter of course at the Hull's or any other's court that if the weather turned sour the racquets were bagged while everyone had tea, cakes, and a lot of shop talk about serves and volleys.

Some of the tennis enthusiasts had done their job well rounding up support for the game, for players soon had the added incentive of competing for trophies. One early donor was Lou Doll, an Eighth Avenue East jeweller. There was a silver Pat Burns challenge cup allegedly valued at nearly $100, and Calgary lumberman W.H. Cushing, the province's public works minister, donated a trophy, as did real estate magnate Fred Lowes.

When the pioneer Prince's Island Tennis Club merged with the Calgary Tennis Club in 1926, the mixed doubles trophy awarded annually by its honorary president, Prime Minister R.B. Bennett, became the joint groups' property. That handsome and venerable cup, its base covered with winners' plaques from half a century of competition, rests in the Glenbow Museum.

Calgary players performed well in tournaments at home and away. Real estate man William Toole brought honours to the Calgary Lawn Tennis Club, winning the Manitoba and Northwest Territories singles title in 1890 and annually from 1893 through 1895. Marjorie Eustace was a consistent titles winner, including nine-time provincial women's singles champion, and has been named to the Alberta Sports Hall of Fame.

In 1912 the Calgary Tennis Club made another move, to the base of the Sunalta escarpment at Fourteenth Avenue and Sixteenth Street SW. This, too, had been CPR property and was spacious enough for the club to lay out six courts surfaced with red Drumheller shale, and a garden, and to erect a roomy clubhouse. It became a showplace and the social centre for Calgary's tennis set.

It had its difficulties, for the organization, with about two hundred members, almost went under in the Depression years. Veteran player and stockbroker Reg Carlile, who had been a member since 1909, was successful in arranging sale of the site to the city and a subsequent leaseback to the membership. Reg, who served the club in many capacities for a quarter of a century, was a dedicated tennis buff. I recall seeing him often, with his short grizzled hair and ramrod bearing, on his three-speed Raleigh bicycle pedalling between his Riverdale Avenue home and the Calgary Tennis Club, with his ever-present racquet and a slicker raincoat strapped to the bike's carrier.

In 1958 the elegant old clubhouse, with its distinctive belfry-capped roof, was destroyed by fire. But the performance of Calgary Tennis Club members remained strong. Between 1930 and 1960, they captured thirty-eight of fifty-four provincial men's and women's singles titles.

Through the 1920s and into the 1930s tennis courts sprouted at places throughout town, such as at: Christ Church in Elbow Park, on the grounds of St. Hilda's Girls' School on Twelfth Avenue West, on New Street, on Twelfth Street east of the Elbow, at Riley Park, Rotary Park, and even in the Scarboro ravine, now buried beneath Crowchild Trail. World War II decimated community tennis groups but over the years hard-surfaced courts, in great part provided by the city, have multiplied and are steadily busy at either end of each long winter.

Getting Technical

*I*t was a day of major disappointment in 1907 when the announcement reached Calgary that the provincial university was to be established in Strathcona, neighbour to Edmonton across the North Saskatchewan River. Politically incompatible with the Liberal government of Premier A.C. Rutherford, Calgarians Dr. T.H. Blow, R.B. Bennett, Thomas Edworthy, William Nimmons, and W.J. Tregillus, all ardent Conservatives, saw their intensive efforts to assemble funding, land, and facilities for a Calgary university come to a halt.

However, for Dr. Blow the crusade was far too intense to be allowed to languish. He devoted most of his time and effort through the years 1910 to 1921 towards the successful establishment of another seat of advanced learning, a technical school. He saw it become a reality in 1916 with the founding of the Provincial Institute of Technology. It was the first of its kind in Canada whose mandate stated that it: " . . . must be based upon, and intimately related to, not only the existing educational system but also the existing commercial and industrial situation."

Because it lacked its own building, the institute opened the doors to its first pupils at Colonel Walker School on Ninth Avenue SE, which housed all grades of public school. A four-room bungalow school, built with federal monies, was erected nearby to accommodate the young pupils, for the school board had passed a resolution in February 1916 stating that "the School Board should enter into an agreement with the Government of Alberta whereby the said board grants the use of the Colonel Walker School buildings and grounds to the Government for a period of four years from January 1, 1916, to be used by the said Government as a School of Technology and Art." On 16 July the transfer took place and veterans of World War I entered the classrooms to be trained for civilian vocations.

That first year the student body consisted of eleven full-time pupils, 195 evening and Saturday morning students, and 150 enrolled in correspondence classes. Additional teaching space was obtained by a takeover of east Calgary's fire and police station. That area was used for training workshops in tractor and automobile mechanics, steam engineering, and metal work.

By 1918, as the scope of training broadened, more civilians than war veterans were enrolled and among the six hundred were some taking Grade Twelve academic subjects and even correspondence courses in coal mining. That year marked the takeover of the school by the federal government, and the doors were opened wide to hundreds of soldiers who were by then returning from armed forces duty and eligible for free tuition. The great strain on facilities created a need for larger premises, and in 1922 the buildings and grounds were returned to the school board, police, and fire departments.

Meanwhile, an impressive three-storey turreted sandstone and brick building arose on the bleak crest of the city's windswept northwest hill. Its cornerstone had been laid by the doggedly determined Dr. Blow, for this was the new home of the institute known affectionately as "the Tech." The 110-acre piece of land previously owned by the Riley family carried a price tag of $63,000 and, in part, was distinguished by a slough that was a favourite winter skating place for north hill families.

There were no entrance exams to the institution, just an age requirement of sixteen, and to some extent it was publicly regarded as a place where misfits in an increasingly academic society went to determine what they might be able to make of themselves by using their hands more than their minds.

A new chapter in the life of the Tech was written with the onrush of World War II. All classes, including those of the Normal School for training schoolteachers, were turfed out of the building which, with hastily built annexes, became RCAF #2 Wireless Training School of the British Commonwealth Air Training Programme. The Tech's temporary home was under the grandstand at the exhibition grounds, now Stampede Park.

One of the institute's outstanding accomplishments reflected Calgary's intense and lasting love affair with aviation. A member of the faculty was Stan N. Green, a former bush pilot who founded, at the Tech, Canada's first school for airframe and motor mechanics. It was the start of something remarkable since, during some of the war years, renowned fighter and bomber aircraft manufacturers in Britain sent staff members over to Calgary for training in Green's classes.

For thirty years Stan Green had nursed a hankering to recreate a spidery high-wing monoplane designed, built, and flown by French pioneer aviator Louis Bleriot. One day, in a secondhand bookstore in Massachusetts, someone ran across a set of plans of the history-making craft Bleriot had flown across the English Channel in 1909.

In November 1952 Green and his students began building an exact replica of the Bleriot flying machine, a task that took them a year. In authentically reproduced detail, powered by an 85-horsepower engine, the 551-pound craft was flown successfully over Calgary by Franz McTavish, a local commercial flyer who had supplied the materials for the project.

To complete his dream, Stan Green shepherded the Tech re-creation to England where it flew the Channel just as the original had done half a century earlier, except this time there was no crash landing to cap the achievement! Perhaps Bleriot, whose family farmed north of Munson near the Red Deer River ferry that bore the family name, would have applauded the student skills for so successfully commemorating his world-famous exploit.

Other accomplishments at the Tech perhaps were less spectacular but its career-building has been enormously successful for thousands of students from Canada and abroad. By 1935, there were as many as forty-eight thousand students; by the 1980s fifty thousand were enrolled in the pioneering school that, in 1961, acquired its present name—the Southern Alberta Institute of Technology—which we all seem to persist in shortening to SAIT.

Its modern role, although embracing the sophistications of this computer age, continues to be one that " . . . manages the planning, development, implementation and improvement of polytechnic education programs and related services, to enable adult Albertans to pursue their personal, social and economic goals through education."

Although currently stated in more complicated language, come to think of it that was the task the original Provincial Institute of Technology was given back in 1916. Those teemingly busy 110 acres on the hill today would make Dr. Blow and his colleagues very proud.

Students and faculty of the Southern Alberta Institute of Technology and Art, as it was called in 1930, pose in front of the original building. Now known as Heritage Hall, this core structure of the vocational school (now known as the Southern Alberta Institute of Technology) was named a national historic site in 1989. **Courtesy Glenbow-Alberta Institute/NA–3900–10**

Fourth Avenue's Elegant Old Lady

Caroline Fulham was the first Calgary woman to assert her position of equality on the local social scene. From her white cottage that once occupied the site of today's court house, she sallied forth loudly with horse and cart to collect hotel kitchen leftovers for her livestock.

More than that, she bellied up to the bar at the Alberta Hotel on Stephen Avenue to demand drinks and conversation on an equal footing with the men, who otherwise dominated the social scene of early Calgary. In my advancing years, that span a considerable portion of our city's history, I have often wished that "Mother Fulham," who was held as a Damoclean threat above our misbehaving young heads years ago ("Behave or I'll give you to Mother Fulham. She'll know what to do with you"), and columnist Suzanne Zwarun could have been buddies in their equality crusade.

However, the uncouth Fulham was looked down upon from a great height by the early women of the town who, by upbringing (and, one hates to think, by choice) were the vassals of the allegedly burly males who created Calgary. Prowling through early records of our city's childhood years, one is hard pressed to find a married woman's Christian name. Mrs. Judge Winter, Mrs. James Lougheed, Mrs. Ezra Riley—all seemed to buckle under the "norm" that, once married, a female became her husband's possession.

Yet, whoever heard of John Fulham? More people remember Maude Riley, Mary Pinkham, Alice Jamieson, and Nellie McClung, who, under their own names, and despite custom, carved niches in Calgary's history. It takes considerable digging to unearth the name of Leonora Christine Woods, who helped found the Young Women's Benevolent Society, bent upon helping destitute "distressed gentlewomen" in Calgary. That is because she was much better known as Mrs. J.H. Woods, he being the general manager and editor of *The Calgary Herald*.

Because of her unmarried state, Miss Annie Elizabeth Mollison was a name synonymous with that of Braemar Lodge, a quiet residential hotel on Fourth Avenue SW. Shrewdly and efficiently she guided the fortunes of that preferred stopping place whose clientele included the most famous names in the theatre. Miss Mollison was also seen every day at the popular afternoon tea gatherings at Braemar Lodge.

Teatime seemed to nourish the inequality of women in those days. The old Sunroom, atop the Palliser Hotel, was another favourite tea-drinking spot. It was soothingly upholstered and decorated in sky blue and ivory—a delightful teacup, cake, and gossip rendezvous high above the city streets. By the way, when an earthquake tickled the city in the early 1930s, plates trembled on the plate rails on the Sunroom walls, creating an unexpected teatime conversation topic.

South of the railway tracks, in Pryce Jones's department store at Twelfth Avenue and First Street SW, ethnically clad waitresses served afternoon tea in the third floor Royal Welsh Tea Room to the accompaniment of a small house orchestra. Rochon's, on Eighth Avenue West, was another well-favoured afternoon tea spot in which I remember wordlessly eating, on the mezzanine level, a hot

This mansion on Fourth Avenue West was built for Calgary's fourth mayor, Daniel Webster Marsh. It later became "Bishop's Palace," the residence of Bishop Cyprian Pinkham of the Church of England. It finished its years as Braemar Lodge, a quiet, dignified residential hotel favoured by visiting theatrical drama troupes. Fire demolished Braemar Lodge in 1965. Courtesy Dr. George Finlay, Calgary

chocolate sundae while my mother and a friend or two chatted about local current events.

Some Calgary women regularly were "at home" to welcome teatime visitors, inviting them by means of small white cards inevitably bearing a name such as Mrs. Herbert Jones.

Afternoon tea, enjoyed by players and their wives, was a ritual, especially at the Calgary Tennis Club and at Riley Park cricket matches. Pound cake, simnel cake, currant buns, biscuits, jams and jellies, and an almost inexhaustible teapot were the ingredients of the gentle afternoon break. A small perforated silver-plated tea ball on a delicate chain or handle was used to keep the leaves captive, unless a teacup-reading fortune teller was on the premises.

The tea maker was required to use clear, cold water and to "always take the pot to the kettle, never the kettle to the pot," for the boiling water had to be bubbling when it hit the tea leaves. One had to feed the teapot "one spoon for each cup and one for the pot." A maidservant had, on the tip of her tongue, the subservient query, "Madam, will I infuse the tea?" at the start of the ceremony.

I clearly recall the sneering disapproval that greeted the appearance of the newly invented tea bag. Never, however, have I been able to fathom the British query, " 'ow abaht a noice cuppa tea?": an assumption that never could there be a nasty one!

Perhaps the afternoon "nice cup of tea" was a very significant part of that gentle elegance of those unliberated women. They might have been found relaxing at the tea table after a serious tussle at whist, five hundred, bezique, or bridge. There would be such as Mrs. Bertram Smith, Mrs. Dr. Mackid, Mrs. George French, Mrs. Reg Peach, Mrs. Charlie Bernard, and Mrs. Colonel Walker. Too many of them were almost nameless, their true potential socially eclipsed by their high-profile husbands.

The Busy Bow

*I*n 1787 explorer David Thompson wintered in the vicinity of a mountain river variously named on subsequent maps the Askow, the Bad and, in Cree, the Manachaben, indicating a stream where evergreen longbow wood grew in abundance.

It took the knowledge of botanist-explorer David Douglas, who entered the mountains some forty years later, to give the trees their official name, Douglas Firs, but the river, source of Indian weaponry, continued to bear the favoured translated name of Bow.

From mountain white-water and moose swamp, past haunts of rainbow and brown trout and mountain whitefish, through sunbaked and naked-antelope country to its swift merging with the South Saskatchewan, the Bow River is only 384 miles long. It was a landmark for explorers and missionaries. Then it began its role as one of the world's busiest streams.

It bore logs from Kananaskis trees cut on its banks to the Eau Claire Mill in Calgary where, during each open-water season, they yielded as many as 5 million board feet of finished lumber annually between 1886 and 1944. Beginning with that first white man's assignment the Bow's responsibilities multiplied. It offered many splendid water power sites, the first of which was in Calgary where, at the turn of the century, a battery of seven water wheels generated electricity for the little city.

In an attempt to even the year-round flow, a wood and gravel barrier meant to tame the Bow was placed just upstream from the mill. In 1909 a full-sized dam was built at Seebe where the Horseshoe power plant became the first of eleven generating stations on the Bow and its tributaries, all west of Calgary.

The river has witnessed a parade of history. In 1832 it saw construction of the Hudson's Bay Company Peigan Post, or Bow Fort, a vain and brief attempt to lure fur traders from Missouri River country before the fort was torched by Indians. It saw the birth and death of Silver City in the shadow of Castle Mountain. Between 1881 and 1886, riverbank Silver City, with a population of three thousand, was the largest settlement between Winnipeg and Vancouver.

Along the convenient Bow River cleft in the Rockies, the Canadian Pacific Railway penetrated the mountain spine of the continent. The river's family of tributaries bears a musical parade of names, among them: Minnewanka, Marvel, Goat, Kananaskis, Spray, Ghost, Jumping Pound, Elbow, Sheep, Arrowwood, and Crowfoot. And there is Bow Lake where it starts, and Hector Lake, Louise, Lac des Arcs, and even San Francisco.

Along most of its brief journey its waters are taken, used, and discarded. Lake Louise, Banff, Canmore, Morley, and Cochrane need some Bow water and, at times, all have cursed and blessed the stream for its seasonal unpredictability. It has been a destructive torrent, a giver of life, an odorous sewer having great difficulty cleansing itself because of the unreasonable demands we place upon it.

Stilled by winter ice it is remembered for the first Banff Winter Carnival in 1917 and, before bridges were built, as a hummock-filled slippery shortcut crossing to Bowness and the Keith Sanatorium. From as far back as 1937 its windswept Ghost Lake has given iceboaters a special thrill and, in summer, has been the sailor's delight.

Bowness Park was land developer John Hextall's gift to the city, created from an island and a Bow River backwater. It was well-maintained by the Calgary Municipal Railway and was a cheap, restful, and picturesque picnic rendezvous for Calgarians, especially during the Great Depression. The charge for everything was a streetcar ticket! Courtesy Glenbow-Alberta Institute/NA–1604–66

One of the biggest Bow River jobs is to help supply Calgary with water and to swill away her wastes. We began drawing water from the Bow in 1913 and today it, and the Elbow, are tapped for about 48 billion gallons annually, returning to the stream below the city approximately 40 billion.

In making its generous donation to our urban well-being the Bow endures some major holdups on its downhill course. In 1929 a mile-long earth, rock, and concrete dam was placed across the stream at its junction with its boisterous tributary, the Ghost. In 1927 the Bearspaw Dam was completed, containing one of the nation's largest pumping stations. Almost a quarter of a century earlier the railway began its irrigation scheme to channel Bow water across parched and potentially productive farm land east and south of the city.

Then the river was dammed at Bassano in 1914 to divert 17 billion gallons of irrigation water annually and was called upon to supply water to the towns of Bassano and Brooks and the villages of Duchess, Rosemary, and Tilley, and the hamlets of Patricia, Rainier, Rolling Hills, and Scandia; and now to towns north of Calgary.

Early in our recorded history, long before it became a major supplier of agricultural water, the river served as a trail marker for settlers, a mecca for ranch herds, and a meeting place at Blackfoot Crossing for the signing of Treaty No. 7. On its way the Bow filled Alberta's largest manmade expanse of water, thirty-four-square-mile Lake Newell, and its latest offspring, the Crawling Valley reservoir.

For all this, the Bow keeps one secret to itself: the timing of those often disastrous spring floods. Once it submerged the old Ghost River highway and bridge during a 1929 weekend. It has lapped doorsteps adjacent to the City Hall, inundated Bowness Park, and submerged St. George's Island and the entire zoo. It has attacked and destroyed an unfinished island filtration plant in Parkdale, and once swept away a whole bridge at Centre Street.

Those were the days before we dammed it and its Minnewanka, Spray, Kananaskis, Ghost, and Elbow tributaries, but we did not begin drinking it until 1972. Pessimistic forecasters love reminding us that the Bow, egged on by the Elbow, has caused $62 million in damage locally during its fits of temper. And despite dams, thirsts, and gloomy crystal-gazing the river continues to taunt us with its secret.

For all its fickle behaviour the Bow River is one of our principal and more beautiful reasons for being here. It deserves more of our careful stewardship, affection, admiration, and respect.

For TLC at Home
You Called the VON

The heart of Ishbel Marjoribanks seems as big as her large, handsome, very womanly body. She was mistress of the vice-regal Ottawa mansion during the term of her husband, the Seventh Earl of Aberdeen (1893–1898), as our governor general.

Throughout those five years she gave liberally of her generosity, compassion, and leadership. While in Canada she created groups such as the Aberdeen Association for the Distribution of Literature to Settlers in the North West. Lady Aberdeen's most impressive Canadian legacy was her creation of the Victorian Order of Nurses, the VON, an organization that is active and highly regarded today, more than ninety years later.

The philanthropic undertaking was fiercely and vocally opposed by the medical profession, whose membership felt the upstart corps of nurses constituted a threat to its monopolistic income and prestige. But the VON, beginning nationally with twelve qualified nurses, received its Royal Charter from Queen Victoria on 28 December 1897 and never looked back.

One of the group's first major undertakings was to organize a team of four nurses to accompany a Canadian government expedition to the Klondike. There, the women established a little hospital and gained the respect of doctors and the rough and tumble population by performing yeoman emergency medical service. Their presence and skills, in primitive frontier circumstances, effectively augmented the efforts of the few overworked doctors during the frenetic and accident-ridden gold rush.

When the Victorian Order of Nurses came to Calgary in 1909 it immediately faced the same sort of medical fraternity hostility as that encountered by VON women in the Klondike. The association of Calgary nurses vigorously resented the VON's intrusion as well, fearful of the erosion of their livelihood. However, gradually the newcomers proved their usefulness by quietly and efficiently filling a gap in local medical-care needs, while being careful not to step on any already established toes.

Funding was a problem from the very start because, in order to establish a Calgary VON branch, the central office in Ottawa required a $500 fee. That problem was met by twenty of Calgary's sixty thousand citizens, each of whom took out five memberships at $5 apiece.

Two weeks later, in September 1909, the Calgary branch of the Victorian Order of Nurses was ready to go to work, backed by an executive and committee consisting of such social lionesses as Mrs. James (later Lady) Lougheed, Mrs. W.R. Hull, Mrs. W.L. Bernard, Mrs. Jean Pinkham and, surprisingly, a pair of won-over male doctors, W.A. Lincoln and G.A. Anderson.

Calgary's first VON nurse was Miss Ethyl Payne, who, with no social or physical anchor, moved away and was replaced by

Opposite: *Local photographer W.J. Oliver took this pre–World War I portrait of the Victorian Order of Nurses, who were performing yeoman service in the small community. With their vehicles, outside their premises at 517 Centre Street South, were: left to right:* Home-visiting VON nurses McKittrick, Ash, Hendrie, Parr, McKee, and Thornton. Courtesy Glenbow-Alberta Institute/NA–1068–1

two registered nurses. A short while later along came Miss Harriet Ash, who instantly identified herself to Calgarians as the VON's high-profile supervisor. She became a familiar figure as she made her rounds by bicycle to visit and attend to tubercular patients, who, back then in 1916, were recipients of very little care and no hospitalization. She and her nursing colleagues operated out of their staff house at 1815 Fourth Street SW.

The VON's mandate was to identify health needs in the Calgary community and, in partnership with other organizations, to provide services and education, preferably in the familiar surroundings of the patients' own home environment.

Calgary's climate was believed to be ideal in aiding recovery from tuberculosis, but regular nursing services and accommodation could not handle the extra load of TB sufferers who descended on our little city before the Central Alberta (later Baker) Sanatorium was built at Keith. Also there was the huge burden placed upon all Calgary medical and nursing personnel by the influenza epidemic of 1918–1919. Here, too, the VON's home-care training and skill were invaluable.

Fortunately the VON acquired an automobile in 1919, sorely needed because maternity work intensified as the city grew and spread over a larger area. In fact, as the VON workload increased, for eight years the Gyro Club underwrote the salary of a new VON baby clinic nurse, the clinic's office expenses, and provided a second automobile.

When the Great Depression clamped its strangle hold on this area the VON almost vanished for want of funds. It was rescued by the generosity of individual Calgarians and the Shriners. Tag days, garden, bridge, and tea parties raised additional funds until, in 1940, the Community Chest (United Way), helped put the VON back on its feet.

Historically, a typical VON annual report—this one happens to cover 1919—revealed the two VON staff members made 3,848 visits, over 2,800 of them being for nursing, 738 for social work, 1,128 of them being free of charge. The two women handled 161 obstetrical cases, 62 child welfare visits, and made 170 night calls. For all of this the organization received, in total fees, $1,119.70.

Today, with the field also served by civic and other care-givers, the VON is very much in the local picture. It welcomes male nurses, and its nineteen full- and part-time registered nurses and home-care health aides make about two thousand visits per month. The dress uniform has changed over the years, but the same compassionate attendance upon those in need still is the job of Lady Aberdeen's Victorian Order of Nurses on the Calgary scene and throughout Canada.

The Lancastrian Left a Large Footprint

*L*ondon-born James Stuart Mackie, Calgary's twelfth mayor, had been a citizen of Calgary for twenty-two years before he delved into real estate development. He had been a successful sporting goods dealer and stationery store proprietor in town, and his first land venture was in 1908 when he built the Mackie Block near the corner of Eighth Avenue and Second Street West.

It was a modest but bold move, for our city's business core clustered in the Centre Street area close to the railway station. Then, in 1911, the city acquired a skyscraper—Mackie's Lancaster Building, an elegant nine-storey business block that sported a generous use of terra cotta and tawny brick, providing a substantial anchor at the west end of our retail and office thoroughfare.

The Lancaster Building site, hitherto a residential lot, initially faced (across Eighth Avenue) the workshop of Head the Plumber and the Jackson Meat Market, until they were replaced in 1912 by the elegant six-floor terra cotta Canada Life Building. To the east (across Second Street) was the Cadogan Block, also erected in 1911, owned by Welsh pioneer R.C. Thomas, on the former site of his Frontier Stables.

In 1914 the Cadogan became the Royal Hotel, the second in Calgary to bear that name. Kitty-corner from the Lancaster at the Second Street and Eighth Avenue intersection was the W.R. Brock wholesale warehouse, stocking draperies, carpets, and dry goods. It was a sombre building with a rooftop water tower.

The small two-storey Mackie office block adjoining the Cadogan is where the ex-mayor and his family lived. As a small boy I fondly remember visiting them. I recall it being such a thrill, in a spread-out little place like Calgary, to be able to visit, and have dinner with, a sophisticated family that actually lived upstairs right in the heart of town. The Mackie boys, Norman and Stuart, older than we, were very gracious and helped us play noisy running games along the corridors, empty in the evening because the commercial tenants had closed for the business day.

Mrs. Mackie, we called her "Aunt" Grace, was a soft, gentle woman. She served wonderful meals in their spacious comfortable apartment, which even had a glass transom above the entry door, and back windows that looked across the low business building roofs all the way to the Bow River and the Crescent Heights cliff.

The Lancaster Building, a couple of doors west, and on the other side of Second Street, was something to make a small boy's mouth gape. It had two elevators, all wrought iron lattice work and brass, and was the centre of the grain trade because brokers had been lured away from W.R. Hull's Grain Exchange Building. One of our dearest family bachelor friends was my father's close buddy, "Uncle" Robin Lethbridge. He worked for the Alberta Pacific Grain Company in the Lancaster Building.

Sometimes we were allowed to visit Uncle Robin as he was winding up his day's business. Occasionally Father would invite him home for supper with us. While Robin cleared away the day's work he would let us play with the tools of his trade on the sloped top of his draftsman-type desk. That is where I discovered a big-cored pencil that wrote blue at one end and red at the other!

James Stuart Mackie was Calgary's very popular mayor in 1901. He built the nine-storey Lancaster building in 1908, an office tower that today is a heritage site; brought provincial and federal officials to examine Calgary as the logical capital of Alberta; and was a prime mover in the building of the Calgary-Edmonton railway. This oil on canvas painting of James Mackie is displayed along with the portraits of other Calgary mayors at City Hall. Artist: Victor Albert Long (1864–1938), Courtesy Glenbow-Alberta Institute/9562

It was in the Lancaster Building in 1925 that I made my first broadcast. The A.P. Grain station, CKLC, had a studio in Edmonton and one in Calgary's Lancaster Building, and its transmitter at Red Deer. It was designed, principally, to broadcast grain prices to country elevator operators and "entertainment" for a small part of the day. It was an office converted into a studio with cloth-draped walls, a microphone, and a baby grand piano, with a "shoe box" of a control room containing the buttons and knobs operated by a man named Foster.

For many years the principal and prestigious tenant of the Lancaster Building's lower floor was Matthews Photo Studio, where the camera artist fussed mightily over his subjects and, in the background, trained his two sons, Peter and John, later camera experts in their own right.

A notable main floor tenant of Mackie's skyscraper was the T. Eaton Company. Between the years 1925 and 1929 it successfully tested the Calgary market by running Eaton Groceteria, a large food market, popular because of its cash and carry service, although its name and merchandising were a direct copy of the sales methods used by Calgary pioneer grocer, Henry Jenkins.

Eaton's later opened its department store a whole block west, labelled a suicidal location since the Lancaster Building was about as far west as anyone went downtown. For a long time the main floor was a very busy drugstore under the Liggett, and then the Tamblyn, banners.

Harold Hanen, architect of our Plus 15 network, told me a while ago that the "skywalks" were a saviour. A strong proposal had been in the wind to demolish the Lancaster. "The implementation of the Plus 15 concept there, linking the Lancaster with TD Square and Scotia Centre, helped the fine old building retain its intrinsic value and enhance its people-use." It seems that, along with the thoughtful cooperation of the Mackie heirs with commercial developers, preserved James Mackie's triumphant achievement.

It May Be Better to Keep Your Tongue in Cheek

Once upon a time there was a cluster of three Bow River islands covered with trees and a tangle of native bushes. It was possible to reach the largest of these islands from the river's south shore through the efforts of a ferryman named W.G. Compton.

The centre of Calgary, in those days, was east of the Elbow's junction with the Bow, so the islands in the river were somewhat of a local attraction. Compton was paid $30 a month for being available to row the ferry boat, which the federal government had established in 1891 for the sum of $160.

There was a certain amount of discussion as to the usefulness of the islands that the feds had leased to Calgary in 1890 for $1 a year each, provided that the town spent at least $100 annually to transform them into a park. In downstream order, St. Patrick's was the first island, followed by St. Andrew's, then the largest, St. George's.

The main island was singled out by an enterprising early Calgarian as a pleasure island. Here a fun-seeking male could pay his fee at a toll booth on the south bank of the river, then cross a footbridge to enjoy himself according to his stamina upon being cheerfully received by a colony of ladies of the night, and for whatever additional joys the other districts of the small town might consider too unsavoury for their neighbourhoods.

In 1908 an iron latticework bridge costing $21,000 was completed across the south branch of the river making St. George's Island, still only partly developed, accessible to the picnicking public. A year later, in 1909, a bandstand was built in the centre of a field that was to become a magnificent green lawn.

During that first summer, free Sunday and evening concerts by the Calgary Scottish Pipers and the Citizens Band played there to large gatherings. The bandstand was a two-storey gingerbread structure, blocky and ornate and fashioned after a German biergarten, although it was consistently denied a beer licence. They served tea there, however, despite the fact that the building trembled alarmingly to the thunderous beat of the outdoor musicians on the upper floor.

As far back as 1913 it was necessary to limit the speed of automobiles on the island to eight miles per hour but the curb was not entirely successful. In 1916 parks superintendent William Reader reported that " . . . there is a tendency for motoring on the island to be abused by speeding, driving on the turf, and into the bushes." Also there had to be considerable policing of picnickers who carelessly lit campfires on the riverbanks.

In October 1928 the Calgary Zoological Society was formed

Opposite: *In 1944 the Calgary Zoological Society began the long high-minded process of "unbarring" the zoo—a painstaking process to house the animals so that they would be more visible to the public, who would no longer have to see the unhappy creatures pacing unrealistically within their cages. Before that happened, one of the minor incidents was a brief and painful encounter through the bars separating Dynamite, a bear, and an adult lion. The disagreement ended when Dynamite, who had derisively stuck out his tongue through the bars at his neighbour, had the tip of it bitten off by the king of beasts.* Courtesy Glenbow-Alberta Institute/NA–2864–2068

and city parks worker Tom Baines became curator of the tiny zoo whose home, it was decided, would be St. George's Island. After a few years they demolished the old bandstand to make way for today's fine big conservatory. At the same time, energetic work was underway to create a natural habitat for the animals, if possible ridding the zoo of its iron bars.

There was a time when the Bow River, on a springtime rampage, threatened the lives of about five hundred zoo creatures. There also was a time when the hazard of barred cages was painfully apparent. One of the larger residents was a Swan Hills grizzly named Dynamite. As a little orphan cub he had wandered onto the frontier homestead of John Aukrenheimer, following him like a dog. Dynamite entertained summer sports crowds by wrestling northern trappers before he grew too big.

The Calgary zoo agreed to accept Dynamite, for a Swan Hills grizzly, the only remaining descendant of the once plentiful huge Plains grizzly, was an endangered species. So the giant beast was brought to the zoo and placed in a cage next to a lion.

The young Swan Hills upstart must have been very rude to the king of the African jungle. One day the bear ambled up to the bars and stuck out his tongue at the lion. In a flash the lion lunged and bit it off. It was a case of yet another emergency call to veterinarian Gordon Anderson, who, for decades, was one of the zoo's most devoted volunteers. Dynamite was tranquillized and operated upon and, despite his unusual handicap, recovered from the unexpected amputation and prospered in captivity until old age caught up to him.

On another occasion Gordon Anderson was called to the zoo to examine an ostrich that was losing its feathers just as winter weather was approaching. Mrs. Lars Willhumsen, the zoo society president's wife, ingeniously knitted a woollen sweater for the bird. Clothing the powerful beast was just one part of the problem. Gordon pored over his medical books, finally determining the ostrich had a nutritional deficiency. Several times he and Tom Baines had to wrestle the angry ostrich to the ground in order to give it vitamin shots in its naked rump. But they won the dangerous skirmishes and later had the thrill of watching pinfeathers sprouting through the bird's knitted sweater.

As a footnote: there was a zoo in Banff until 1937 when it was closed. Willhumsen persuaded senior Boy Scouts of the Fourth Calgary Rover crew, with the help of the Elks Club, to truck the animals, including a polar bear, to Calgary, thus ending the nightly howling at passing trains. I don't know about Banff nowadays but nights are said to be really quite quiet down there on St. George's Island.

Home Sweet Home

A prehistoric peninsula that thrusts itself from the southwest into the lake that once filled today's Bow/Elbow valley, is known today as the hill of Mount Royal. It is bounded on the north by the Seventeenth Avenue area, on the east by Cliff Bungalow, and on the south by inundating contours, including the Premier, Council Way, and Harvie Park coulees, until the valley of the Elbow is reached.

The potential of the northern slope was spotted early in Calgary's history by its owner, the Canadian Pacific Railway. The company invested considerable effort in promoting the hillside as prospective high-class residential property even though, in those days, it was a considerable distance by horse and carriage from Calgary's centre of business and residential activity.

The price tag of land on the hillside was around $20 per acre and, at that price, my father bought a plot well beyond the crest of the hill. He chose it because it sloped southward to a creek that had carved itself a twisting coulee down to the Elbow River. The land was well removed from either of the rivers that had a nasty habit of flooding the lowlands, yet a tiny bridge he built across the creek was a picturesque addition to the stately house and its slanting forefront. In time that creek was harnessed in a large buried pipe beneath the winding paved road that was named Premier Way.

The sales pitch for home building on that entire hill was aimed chiefly at well-to-do Americans who were looking for cheap land, elbow room, loose social and legal shackles in a new country, and a chance to make a quick fortune in cattle and real estate. One result was that the east end of the northward slope, between what became Eighth Street and the Cliff Bungalow area, earned the nickname of American Hill. It was a boulder-strewn stretch of sloping prairie, so another result was a plethora of rock walls and fences, many of which are very much in evidence today. In fact, for a time, the bald-headed hillside sprouted far more mansions and harsh-looking rocky boundaries than greenery, for every tree now clothing Mount Royal had to be hand-planted.

Pioneer merchant David Jackson Young, whose mansion and adjacent coach house still stand on the Eighth Street hill, moved his family into their new home in 1909. Behind their property they pastured their cow and two horses, and in the coach house they made room for their 1911 Cadillac, Calgary's first automobile with electric headlights.

One of their neighbours, where Amherst Street forks southeastward from Eighth Street, was Dr. Thomas H. Blow, who fathered the technical school we know as SAIT. His huge, square-towered, red brick mansion had a panoramic view of the little city, as did the stately homes of many other new Calgarians who chose Mount Royal. The Blow house is another that still stands, although it is increasingly hemmed in as the hillside area becomes more and more financially precious.

When the hillside was first surveyed the railway gave it the name of Mount Royal because so many of the company's officials hailed from Montreal. Between 1909 and 1914 the area was a beehive of construction, every site containing a dwelling of mansion calibre. Local sandstone was a favourite building material, although a lavish use of brick and half-timbering on stucco gave the upbeat district a handsomely varied ambience.

Highly successful liquor merchant Vital Raby, late of Montreal, was one of the early residents of the lower Mount Royal hillside, while financial broker T.J.S. Skinner in 1911 built his imposing mansion on a large and lavishly landscaped corner property near the top of the hill on Hope Street and Prospect Avenue. Lawyer R.B. Bennett, who was to become our prime minister, had a Prospect Avenue address and so did New York-born Charles Traunweiser, hotelier and livestock man, who, in 1912, chose locally made tawny brick for his stately home.

On Hillcrest Avenue, just over the top of the hill, were the big homes of Scottish newspaperman Malcolm Geddes, and sporting goods merchant Alex Martin. In time the big Martin house, bought by the Anglican Church, became known as Bishop's Palace. In all, Mount Royal, right from the start, was an imposing architectural showplace.

In 1912 the street railway planners proposed laying tracks up Eighth Street, then west along Prospect Avenue to link with the South Calgary loop line at Fourteenth Street West. Despite the popularity of streetcars at that time, and the petitioned approval of Mount Royal property owners, the line was never built. Actually, though, in 1935 Mount Royal became the designated route of our first modern motorbuses.

The name link between the area and Mount Royal College was formed in 1910 when the institute's founder, Dr. George Kerby, was being pressured by the provincial premier for a name. With Dr. Rutherford on the long distance line from Edmonton, Kerby looked up from his desk, which faced the hillside. He is said to have answered the impatient premier with "All right, call it Mount Royal College." Thus, almost by accident, the name of the local seat of learning became irrevocably enjoined to Calgary's first top-ranking residential area.

Opposite: In Calgary's early years, around the turn of the century, the city contained a large number of elegant mansions, many of them built with local sandstone. Although Mount Royal became the most popular address of the newly arrived wealthy, including future prime minister R.B. Bennett, some prosperous Calgarians settled on Fourth Avenue West, nicknamed "Millionaires Row." South of the railway was the home of Senator Pat Burns; "Beaulieu," the stately home of Senator Sir James Lougheed; and William Roper Hull's home "Langmore" (pictured here). Courtesy Glenbow-Alberta Institute/NC–24–169

Dirty Hands Created
Full Tummies

*A*n idea, however inspired, does not have to be born of exotic circumstances. In this case an admirable inspiration, while neither original nor glamorous, certainly emerges from prosaic roots.

The "ingredients" are a pail of manure, horse-loving Ca Lorraine Taylor, and Calgary's depressed economic malaise that has created a need for soup kitchens and food banks for citizens in straitened circumstances. Together they create a civic challenge unmatched since the days of the Great Depression and the perilous conditions created by World War II. Having been overseas during that war, I was unable to recall the crisis of the 1940s. However, I do clearly remember the impact of the 1930s Depression that resulted in scores of Calgarians toiling with spades, forks, and rakes on our vacant lots.

You see, Lorraine, who boards her horses a few miles from Calgary, asked the farm proprietor for a pail of manure to bring back to the city to fertilize her garden. "If you have a pick-up," he urged, "bring it out and I'll gladly give you a truckload." So she and I got talking on the phone of the days when Calgary's transportation ran on hay and oat horsepower rather than on gasoline and diesel fuel.

Cartage companies, corner store retailers, departmental and small customer delivery services, the city's garbage and street cleaning and maintenance crews all used horses. It was a boon for gardening Calgarians, including our parks department. The big busy stockyard's four-legged transients produced railcars of potential fertilizer that found its way, in trainload lots, to a huge dump at the corner of the present Canyon Meadows Drive and the Macleod Trail. That's where low-income Calgarians mingled with gourmet mushroom-pickers during the warmer seasons to augment their family menus.

In still earlier years, curb-side water troughs were thoughtfully placed throughout the city core for the cart horses of those days, as there were busy farriers and stables. Blacksmiths and local foundries turned out the iron weights known as tether blocks, halter shanks, or tether weights, to deter harnessed work horses from straying, driverless, along bread, milk, and ice delivery routes.

And all the while, in those days before "natural food" fads, gardeners made good use of the animals' droppings, knowing the nutrition they would impart to their plantings. Another good soil conditioner was a crop of potatoes, and in 1911, to provide a suitable base for future lawns on St. George's Island, the city planted enough potatoes to fill six hundred sacks, which were then donated to hospitals and the Calgary needy.

The World War I manpower drain inspired the creation of a Vacant Lots Garden Club, which in turn inspired the city to

Opposite: *During World War I it was considered a patriotic gesture on the part of citizens as well as the City Park Department to use vacant city land for growing vegetables. The habit continued through the Great Depression. The crops were donated to jobless families from the city as well as to institutions. Here a large vegetable patch, planted west of the General Hospital in the Riverside district, covered acres of vacant land (circa 1920).* Courtesy Glenbow-Alberta Institute/16–04–76

cultivate more than 250 empty building lots and make them available to needy citizens and volunteer gardeners. Every one of those lots produced a crop that first year and the yield included potatoes, beets, beans, peas, cabbage, cauliflower, carrots, turnips, parsnips, squash, some berry bush fruits, strawberries, and rhubarb.

Following that harvest the city readied 134 vacant lots for the next year's planting. In 1915, war-decimated family incomes and a rise in the cost of living made vacant lot gardening all the more valuable, so the city encouraged its development by donating three hundred bushels of seed potatoes to the needy.

In 1917, many ex-soldiers sought to reestablish their livelihoods upon their return from European battlefields by trying their hands at gardening. That year the city cultivated over three hundred vacant lots at no charge to the users. The War Veterans Association distributed another gift from the city, six hundred bushels of seed potatoes. One such venture on about two hundred acres of vacant land near the General Hospital produced over two thousand bushels of potatoes and hundreds of pounds of other vegetables. Even land along what is now Memorial Drive, and parts of Mewata and Riley parks, were planted in vegetables for the use of charitable institutions and hospitals.

Today we hear a lot of nonsense about the dearth of vacant land in our city. We also hear a lot about the urgent requirements of the food banks and soup kitchens. Many farmers on Calgary's outskirts are "up to here" in—let's not offend anyone—"herd droppings." There is considerable unemployed male and female muscle out there, too.

Each time we start back up the slope of the year towards the growing season, the "ingredients" are there. And remember, Christmas never seems far away, and sure enough, in due course along will come another Season to be Jolly with Cauli.

Streetcars and the End of an Era

*I*n 1950 the last streetcar run marked the end of a splendid urban transportation chapter in Calgary's history.

The system started its era of service on 5 July 1909, beginning with two streetcars, three miles of track, and sixteen employees. One terminus of the first route was the newly built streetcar barns on the north bank of the Elbow River on the west edge of Victoria Park's exhibition grounds. The "downtown" end of the tracks was at First Street West and Eighth Avenue.

The shrewdly timed inauguration of the streetcar service was during Exhibition Week, and visitors stood shoulder-to-shoulder along the two-mile route to cheer the first car on its way. The most exciting part for them was to see Car No. 1 successfully grind through the Second Street East subway under the CPR tracks. The ease with which it negotiated the slopes confounded critics who had predicted it couldn't be done.

The inaugural run was made with several VIPs aboard including Mayor Reuben R. Jamieson and commissioners A.G. Graves and S.J. Clarke and Street Railway Superintendent T.H. McCauley. The motorman was Charles Comba, who returned the cheers of the onlookers with toots of the streetcar's air whistle and the clanging of its bell. That Exhibition Week the original pair of streetcars

unwittingly became one of the fair's great attractions and thirty-five thousand fare-paying passengers tried out the trams!

The vehicle that rolled along the rails first was built by an Ottawa car company: a sixteen-wheeler, built of wood, with woven wicker-covered seats and a thirty-six passenger capacity. With the diverting excitement of the exhibition behind them, Calgarians soon had an enthusiastic love affair going with the Calgary Municipal Railway's noisy, lumbering vehicles. Garishly painted a sort of orange-red with cream trim, the eight- and four-wheeled trams penetrated most corners of the little city and for years enjoyed having earned the greatest rider approval of any street railway in Canada.

Typical of the system's record-breaking growth were the 1910 tally in which the year-old carrier had eighteen cars and twenty-two miles of track and, only a year later, forty miles of route serviced by thirty cars. By the Calgary Municipal Railway's third anniversary, in 1912, fifty-seven cars of various types ran along sixty miles of track.

Not everyone was a friend. The Reverend George Kerby, pastor of Central Methodist Church at First Street West and Seventh Avenue, tried without success to have Sunday streetcar traffic abolished, but he was vigorously opposed by both daily newspapers. A few years later, when the system was expanding at a great clip, a line was proposed running south from Seventeenth Avenue, up Eighth Street in Mount Royal, then west along Prospect Avenue to link with the Fourteenth Street hilltop loop of the South Calgary route. Residents there were successful in actively rejecting the idea. But in those days gone by, before most families had an automobile, residents of some suburban districts were engaged in spirited competition for the prestige and convenience of having a streetcar line running along the middle of their street.

One very welcome service made it possible for scores of blue-collar workers residing in east Hillhurst (New Edinburgh, as it was called for a while) to reach their workplace in Ogden, far off to the southeast. The inauguration of streetcar service to the site of the Canadian Pacific Railway shops under construction had been one of the selling points in having the railway establish its very large locomotive and car building and repairing complex here rather than in Medicine Hat or Bassano. Of course it turned out to be a great blessing during two world wars when, each time, Ogden Shops became a builder of heavy armaments for the Allied Forces.

That Ogden tram route got off to a bit of a shaky start. The inaugural streetcar run took place on 31 December 1912 while the "Mountain Shops" were under construction. When the opening took place the following March, the Calgary Municipal Railway found it needed more streetcars to adequately serve the five hundred or more workers. Public tours were conducted to mark the opening of the Ogden Shops. The trams were adequate for those very large crowds but transporting the employees daily was another matter. However, the railway stepped in temporarily and ran workers' trains between Ogden and downtown Calgary at either end of each working day until the streetcar people were able to take over the job. That they did with special double-header trams at rush hour, plus an hourly service beginning at 6:30 A.M. each weekday.

There was more than a touch of sadness when Calgary's streetcar service came to an end on 29 December 1950, to be replaced by trolley buses and diesel-powered motorbuses. That final run was made from the loop outside the gates of Ogden Shops by streetcar #14 with operator R. Thompson at the controls. Partway into the city Thompson moved aside to allow a very special passenger to sit on the driver's stool. It was retired Calgary Municipal Railway Superintendent Charles Comba, who had driven the very first car in 1909. Also on board the inbound run from Ogden was retired Commissioner Arthur Graves, a passenger, just as he had been on the inaugural run years earlier. Mayor Don Mackay was another rider and, before the trolley pole was lowered and the lights went out, a small crowd of streetcar buffs and city officials sang "Auld Lang Syne."

For some years car #14 sat decaying on Calgary Brewing Company property, for there were plans afoot to establish some sort of museum there. But #14 was given rebirth. Combining the original frame and a pair of electric power trucks obtained from the Toronto Transit Commission, a replica of a car of the once-booming street railway system was re-created.

Workmen at Heritage Park painstakingly built the tram to the specifications of its original builder. Out there it is dressed in the old familiar Calgary Municipal Railway livery and, at the front, wears a moustache-like cowcatcher that once was so necessary when indeed Calgary was a cowtown. Heritage Park people are the deserving custodians of the lone fully operational relic of a busy fleet of Calgary's very successful people-movers.

Opposite: *For forty-one years Calgarians, in a constantly growing and spreading city, were served during peace and war by a very efficient, electric streetcar system. Residents of some districts enthusiastically welcomed the convenience of the electric cars; other areas wanted no part of the noisy intrusion. One churchman tried to have Sunday streetcar service suspended because its proximity disturbed his sermons.* Courtesy Provincial Archives of Alberta/H. Pollard Collection/P4030

The Picture Palace
with Its Silver Screen

*T*he last of Calgary's imposing movie houses has reached the end of the line. The Palace Theatre, for seventy-one years an ornamental resident on the south side of Eighth Avenue—the Stephen Avenue Mall—is dead.

In 1919 the Allen Palace opened its ornate doors to offer Calgarians first-run silent movie fare in an almost regal ambience. Only one other movie house threatened to eclipse the Palace when, in 1921, the Capitol opened on the north side of the same block. However, by that time the Palace was solidly established as a premium quality film and vaudeville showplace.

Planners are struggling to find a solution to the now somewhat tacky evening appearance of our one-time "main street." Perhaps, understandably, they overlook that fact that it was Eighth Avenue's large family of movie houses with brilliant marquee lighting and flashing signs that brightened the thoroughfare as only the garish movie house showmanship could accomplish.

The Palace Theatre was in the forefront. Running lights chased each other around the marquee advertising, under which people lined up at the brilliantly lit box office to see the first-run films from the best loge seats in the house—with smoking privileges—for 50¢.

Between acts and show times the mighty pipe organ, played by Ted Forsey, thunderingly entertained Palace patrons in the 1,784 plush-upholstered seats. Radio-Keith-Orpheum and Pantages circuits, rivals in peddling top-rated live acts, battled for bookings. Beneficiaries of their striving were the Palace Theatre customers.

The uninhibited manager of the Palace was Winnipeg-born Pete Egan, a genius of gimmickry to capture full houses for every new entertainment bill. The cheerful, bustling, innovative manager was everybody's friend but Pete's great ally, according to his son Carl, was a book called *The Motion Picture Encyclopedia of Exploitation*. Carl told me his father issued him a challenge: if he could come up with a customer-baiting stunt that wasn't in that book, Pete would pay his lad $10, a princely sum at the time. Carl never collected.

The Calgary Symphony Orchestra conducted by Grigori Garbovitsky performed regularly at the Palace with such luminaries as Jascha Galperin, whose violin performances were as fiery as his red hair. A young violinist named Jean de Rimanoczy achieved western Canadian fame there long before receiving international acclaim with the Seattle Symphony.

Beginning one Sunday in November 1925, Crescent Heights High School principal William Aberhart made his first nervous appearance before an uncompromising microphone and a full-house audience to begin spreading, by radio, the Social Credit gospel that finally landed him in the legislature.

The Palace was chosen for the world premiere showing of *His Destiny*, a Calgary Stampede and Brooks, Alberta, area horse opera

Opposite: The Palace Theatre (originally the Allen Palace) on Eighth Avenue was the height of opulence for a first-run movie house. Its stage was used by many artists, including Victor Borge. The Palace became the Sunday meeting place for William Aberhart, high school teacher and gospel preacher who turned politician and premier. Courtesy Glenbow-Alberta Institute / NA–1178–2

No 1.

starring Neal Hart and Alberta's own movie star, Barbara Kent. But it was up to Pete Egan to come up with one of the truly madcap stunts to publicize his movie house and its screen and stage offerings. He had a Calgary bodyshop weld, back-to-back, the front halves of two Ford coupes. Until discouraged by the unsmiling police, he shuttled along Eighth Avenue in this weird billboard that could bewilderingly change direction, touting the great shows at "Calgary's Friendly Theatre."

In late 1938 the Palace and the Capitol issued Moviescope, a small eight-page free flier. It advertised main floor seat admission, at either theatre, for 27¢ until 5:30, and smoking in loge seats, amusement tax included. Evening prices rose to the dizzy heights of 38¢ and 50¢.

In addition to the regular fare, the Palace offered personal appearances of local artists such as piano accordionist Stan James with vocalist Jack Lee. Both also were a part of "Shadowland," a regular promotion show sponsored by the Palace on radio. Pete's son Gail Egan, who was a sports radio commentator, was host of the theatre's series.

Several Moviescope ads were deliberately missing some letters in their script. If you sent the nearest correct answer spotting the omissions you would be eligible for a gift from Temple Duff, a drug company sharing the same block of Eighth Avenue.

The Palace offered free checking of coats and parcels while patrons watched the show. In the check room at all times was "a qualified matron with complete First Aid Kit" and as a "Service For Doctors: the ushers are equipped with cards to record the names and seat numbers of professional men and others who might be expecting telephone calls while in the theatre." Pete explained privately that, in large part, this was his insurance against a favourite ploy used by doctors to spread free publicity among those in an audience by being paged by name during performances.

With the theatre's passing is an era of filmdom that, in this same year of the requiem of the passenger train, marks the end of another piece of leisurely elegance sentenced to genocidal oblivion by today's version of civilization. Rest in Peace, Palace Theatre—has anyone got a hanky?

Blossoms and Greenery under Glass

*T*here was a time when, throughout our small city, acres of glass trapped Calgary's annual average of over twenty-three hundred hours of sunshine. Its nurturing warmth for plants and seedlings proved alluring to many early businessmen with "green thumbs" whose commercial greenhouses flourished.

On the edge of town was the brand new southern suburb of Rideau beyond the village of Rouleauville and the wooden span of the Mission Bridge over the Elbow River. There, in 1897, in what was to become a coveted residential neighbourhood enhanced—and occasionally menaced—by the nearness of the river, John Emery set up his greenhouse. He was good at building glass houses, for he had been a glazier at Cushing brothers' east Calgary sash and door factory.

The Calgary Greenhouses was the name of Emery's new enterprise covering about two-and-a-half acres under eleven thousand square feet of glass. Soon he was able to supply the Calgary market, and a good many out-of-town mail order customers, with cut flowers, bulbs, and house plants. He had also opened a retail store at Twelfth Avenue and First Street West.

Financial difficulties forced Emery to sell out to the Hammond Floral Company, which carried on the business in that quiet suburb. Some years later the Whitburn family took over the thriving enterprise, conducting it until the 1980s when the land became more valuable as residential lots than as one of Calgary's principal sources of floral supplies.

About 1903 a greenhouse had been built on a piece of open land at Sixth Avenue and First Street West by the Terrill brothers from Prince Edward County, Ontario. Alfred and John Terrill had learned their professional greenhouse operational skills from their gardener and fruiterer father.

After several successful years, while Calgary's downtown area experienced a fast and intensive period of growth, the Terrills were compelled to move. Their landlord was Senator James Lougheed, who wanted to erect on the property a business block and theatre, his Lougheed Building and the Grand Theatre that was to nestle within it. So, far from the centre of town, at Ninth Avenue and Sixteenth Street SE, the Terrills constructed 225,000 square feet of greenhouses where, for example, between 1921 and 1970, they hosted the annual Chrysanthemum Tea amid the acres of blossoms.

Thomas Riley, the rancher who gave Calgary twenty-acre Riley Park in Hillhurst, had sold some of his land that hugged the base of the hill to the Campbell Floral and Seed Company, which became another large commercial greenhouse firm. Before long that sprawling business at Sixteenth Street and Eighth Avenue NW maintained acres of growing space under glass.

By that time the prairie sun glinted off the glass roofs of greenhouses in several parts of the city. On Fourth Street NW we used to wander through the large glass-roofed greenery at Pederson's and, on the north bank of the Bow River near the Langevin Bridge, through the Sunnyside growing-under-glass establishment.

Nowadays one must search for the gleam of commercial greenhouse roofs, for very few remain within the city limits. The large multi-paned sun-catchers of today are scattered in such places as Balzac, Standard, Okotoks, Strathmore, Midnapore, and Springbank.

Under his years of leadership, renowned city parks head William Reader saw to it that a civic greenhouse was established three-quarters of a century ago close by the old arched Union Cemetery entrance. It was a busy place with an annual production of forty thousand bedding-out plants that beautified our city parks.

In his 1917 annual report William Reader noted that "flowers have been sent regularly to the General, Holy Cross, Tuberculosis and Isolation hospitals, Children's Aid, and Convalescent Home." According to parks chronicler Morris Barraclough, plants were loaned for decorative purposes at all kinds of functions, and over twenty-five hundred plants were sold to local florists, resulting in a revenue of $500. One of William Reader's goals was to expand the city enterprise in 1918 and make the greenhouse self-supporting.

In 1923, as a budgetary saving, city council decided to operate the greenhouse for only six months of the year, whereupon former city parks department gardener William Stark, who had operated that city greenhouse from its 1911 opening, leased the facility and operated it as his own commercial business for the next eighteen years. Of course that greenhouse site has been obliterated by the north portal of the Light Rapid Transit tunnel beneath Cemetery Hill.

I regard, as one of our more intelligent architectural acquisitions, the business office tower atrium—a sort of a token miniature representation of our big St. George's Island Conservatory. In this so frequently hostile climate, the office block with its multi-storeyed atrium roof glass between us and our generous southern Alberta sunlight is one of our better environmental achievements in the recent past.

Opposite: *Calgary's altitude, latitude, and meagre annual precipitation have enhanced the growing of decorative plants under glass. One of the earlier greenhouses was built in the first decade of this century for the City Parks Department. Located at the foot of "Cemetery Hill," it grew plants for the cemetery gardens and small city-owned parks scattered about the city. Large commercial greenhouses have always done a "bargain day" volume of business, particularly during our short growing season.* Courtesy Glenbow-Alberta Institute/NA–2423–5

The Naked Truth
Is Not Immodest

I was pleased when the Tom Campbell Hill was endorsed by the city planning commission as a community green space. It had been a long process for some of the residents. They had been striving to head off a proposal to convert the commanding hilltop into view-point residences for a few, rather than a panoramic open area for the many.

The earliest local map in my possession, dated 8 March 1884, indicates the hilltop as part of a ranch owned by pioneer Cuthbert McGillis, whose property spanned the Nose Creek Valley and spread up to the crest of the hill. More than that, the empty prairie was diagonally dissected by a northwest-southeast Indian trail.

A 1911 map shows part of the hilltop, not quite reaching the lip of the hill, as being laid out in a few oblong, but unsurveyed, building lots. Then, a year later those lots were surveyed, but the area had yet to be given its original name of St. George's Heights. Next, a roadway named St. George's Drive, with a panoramic view, appeared to curve near the scenic edge of the area.

The hill, after centuries of having been part of the steep northern bank of the lake that filled the basin of Calgary, was left high and sandy dry by the receding Ice Age glacial waters and wound up dipping its sandy toe in the Bow River.

Indians from the Gleichen area, trudging to their trading and hunting partners in the eastern Rockies, had a choice of three mountain-bound routes. One was uphill to the flatland above the Bow, then northwest to Morley, and The Gap, and beyond. Another was to gingerly skirt the sometimes flooded base of the hill at the shoreline of the river. The third crossed the Bow at its shallowest and aimed at the mountains in a southwesterly course, today, Richmond Road and out to Bragg Creek and Eden Valley country. The Indians' three-pronged route was known as the Blackfoot Trail. When horse-drawn wagon traffic made its appearance, a cart track around the base was chopped back a bit to make a shelf along which settlers could travel above the water level.

As Calgary grew, so its merchants set up shop. One of them was Tom Campbell, a hatter. He placed a very large billboard on the edge of the hilltop in plain sight of just about everyone in little Calgary. From 1912 to 1948 that sign was a landmark urging men to wear "Smile" hats made by the Tom Campbell Hat Company.

It was the era of the Kewpie Doll, naked, pot-bellied, with stubby wings at the shoulder blades, twinkling eyes, and a perennial grin. Tom Campbell's graphic artist depicted a nude Kewpie child in a much-oversized silk top hat, holding a swagger cane strategically sloped for the sake of decency. The message was, "Wear a Tom Campbell Hat and Smile!" and the non sequitur, "The Naked Truth Is Not Immodest."

Opposite: *Residents of the Tom Campbell Hill recently won a long squabble with the city to have the flat-topped acreage above Memorial Drive (seen in the right foreground of the photo) designated as a natural prairie park. For a while it was a fenced area for the zoo's ungulates, whose carefree, uninhibited behaviour offended those who lived on the hilltop. At last the householders are at peace with nature!* Courtesy Glenbow-Alberta Institute/NA–5093–411

But immodesty did appear in 1910 when, in order to avoid annoying city restrictions, Calgary's principal red light district moved around the corner of the hill beyond the city limits. There, near the mouth of Nose Creek, stood a cluster of well-patronized pleasure houses.

Herb Higgs, an elderly car salesman, had fun telling me that, as a boy, he occasionally played hooky from school to drive a hired horse and buggy for the enterprising owner of a Calgary livery stable. One day his fares were a certain flouncy Miss Irene and her wealthy john. Herb was instructed to drive them around the base of the hill and out of town to the romantic Nose Creek rendezvous.

He galloped his rig into town clutching the totally extravagant $10 tip. Unluckily, back at the stable, he bragged excitedly of this new way of making money to a policeman who knew his father. Herb was allowed to keep the $10 but, because of his youth, was warned by the policeman, his employer, and his father never to drive people out that way again.

Between the years 1959 and 1984 passion again invaded old St. George's Heights. The Calgary Zoological Society was permitted use of the Tom Campbell Hill as a paddock for a number of hoofed animals such as zebras, camels, antelopes, and llamas. The "doin'-what-comes-naturally" romantic shenanigans of these imported lovers roused the ire of some twittery residents of the hilltop to great heights of indignation.

During these same years, part of this "passion pasture" was chopped to make way for a widening of Memorial Drive. Then more of the hill's edge was pared when the northeast leg of the Light Rapid Transit was installed along the foot of Tom Campbell Hill.

But now, at long last, high above the din of Memorial Drive rail and road traffic, the top of one of Calgary's most renowned hills is bound to restore itself in peace as an inner city wildlife area, to give pleasure to all.

Boy Scout Bird Box Builders

*I*t was heart-warming to read of the "Bird Man of Cochrane," Blake Stillings, who is reported to have installed more than four hundred birdhouses north of Cochrane especially for bluebirds, which seem rare in the city nowadays.

They were the symbol of a ripened spring in my young days and, always, we hoped they would become tenants of the scores of birdhouses we built as members of the Tenth Troop of Boy Scouts.

For all our fervour we had scant knowledge of the fine art of birdhouse construction. I, as the son of a building contractor, had my own set of tools, albeit blunt, much worn, and at least second-hand. So I fancied myself no end as a well-intentioned, even skilled, member of the troop.

It was an annual undertaking of the senior members of Scout-master Leslie Sara's Roxboro and Rideau Park troop. Most bird-house building was done during the winter in our basements at home. With that completed, we met at the hall on Rideau Road, loaded with our prideful accomplishments, then set off for one of three springtime project locations.

One was the bird sanctuary we of the Tenth established on the midstream Elbow River Island, a steppingstone for the Mission Bridge. Our dedicated and successful aim was to protect the island and to supply birdhouses. The island was known as Swastika, long before the ancient good luck talisman was disgraced by Hitler. However, years ago, the Tenth lost title to the island to Marathon Realty.

As for our second goal, today, driving along Twelfth Avenue West, past our one-time main public library, I marvel at the enormous, venerable trees lining the north edge of Memorial Park. In the days when it was the newly planted Central Park, those giants of today were tender saplings.

In order to reach their upper finger-thick branches, we had to use a stepladder—they were too young and wobbly to stand the weight of a leaning ladder. Carefully we would secure one of our home-made birdhouses in the sparse shelter of each sapling's twig leaves feeling we were contributing mightily to little Calgary's songbird population.

In the autumn we would gather again in the basement shop of the librarian's grounds-keeper. In the chill of a frosty Saturday, we would take down each birdhouse, empty, and clean it. Every weather-worn little structure was then destined for Scouts' basements for refurbishing in time for the following spring. The library caretaker's workbench, tools, nails, and paint pots were always at our springtime disposal for last-minute touchups or strengthening.

Each spring we added to the number of birdhouses as the trees became sturdy enough to support them. One year a short, tubby cameraman with a French accent, Lucien Roy of Fox Movietone News if I remember correctly, was on the scene filming, in silent black and white, our endeavours.

Weather permitting, five of us senior scouts of the Tenth spent the following three Saturdays at Keith Sanatorium for tuberculosis patients. Keith was the name of the railway whistle-stop well patronized for decades before the Eighty-fifth Street bridge was erected across the Bow River in 1961.

We loved the train trip out there and back, for it was the third stop west of the city in those far-off days, making it a rail journey of some substance. Everyone called it the Keith San, although for thirty-two years the post Great War institution was headed by Dr. Albert Baker, who was himself a TB sufferer at one time. After his death it was renamed the Baker Memorial Sanatorium.

Here, too, the newly planted saplings were barely robust enough to hold birdhouses in safety. The clutch of pavilions stood on a barren stretch of prairie across the river from the forest-covered Bowness Park. During the San's first years it was far too bleak a setting to attract birds for the pleasure and companionship of the long-term patients. Each year we would set out thirty or more birdhouses amid merry shouted heckling from the lonely patients looking down on us from the screened balconies of their pavilions.

My right thumb still has a souvenir of those Keith birdhouse days—a thin scar. It is a reminder of the need to be careful of the razor-sharp blade of a Scout pocketknife. It "won" me a trip to the Keith infirmary where it was mended despite my fears of catching "a case of TB!" On each of the four or five yearly visits the Scouts made to the Keith, we were sombrely warned never to touch a patient lest we catch the dreaded malady that was claiming the lives of so many Albertans.

I often wondered if the birds talked about us and our efforts, back in the 1930s, as enthusiastically as we did about our adventures among the young branches on Swastika Island, and at Central Park and Keith, opposite Bowness. Today I suppose we'd be called some sort of amateur environmentalists. In those days we were a few kids who liked to hear the uninhibited songs of wild birds.

Opposite: *Boy Scouts of the Tenth (Rideau) Calgary Troop specialized in building and placing birdhouses in trees in Calgary's parks and along some residential streets. This photo, taken in the late 1920s, shows the lads installing some of their hobby handiwork in Garden Crescent, Elbow Park.* Courtesy Glenbow-Alberta Institute/NA–4487–4

Central School—
Now an Oasis, a Cupola,
and a Memory

*T*here is a city block in our business centre that will become an interesting blend of the earliest and the latest of a 108-year span of Calgary history.

In 1883 that property was owned by Edward Baynes, one of thirty-two homesteaders who chose the Bow Valley as a place to raise a family, keep livestock, and grow grain. A portion of his land today is bounded on the north and south by Fourth and Fifth avenues and, on the east and west, by Centre Street and First Street SW.

Central School arose on that block in 1887, a two-storey wooden building housing four classrooms in which pupils were taught between the hours of 9 A.M. and 4 P.M. in circumstances that soon were far from ideal. Calgary's growth was swift and soon one of the classrooms was jammed with 113 pupils. Some drastic action was called for.

In January 1889 Ontario-born James Short, a twenty-seven-year-old teacher with aspirations of becoming a lawyer, was appointed principal at a salary of $1200 per year. His major task was to organize our city's first high school in that midtown building.

In 1903 construction began on a new, larger, $59,000 Central High School a few yards to the west of the original building. Dignified in appearance and three storeys in height, it was constructed of local sandstone, and its roof crowned with a large ornamental metal cupola with provision for a four-faced clock. Then, during World War I, the original Central was demolished and the entire area surrounding the sandstone Central School became a much-trampled grassless playground.

James Short was the school's principal for only four years during which time, in 1890, he was given the added task of school board secretary with an additional salary of $50 per year.

In 1892 Short almost blotted his copybook, for he was charged with having struck a boy and two girls with his hand and allegedly threatening to flog another girl for misbehaving.

James Short was declared innocent of all but one accusation. He had indeed "acted injudiciously in striking the boy with his hand, as he admitted he did . . . " It was a prickly gathering, especially with the boy's irate father present. However, the trustees were convinced by the evidence that the lad " . . . had given his teachers much trouble and annoyance and was deserving of punishment."

Short changed careers and was admitted to the bar in 1895, although he continued to serve on the Calgary School Board and the Educational Council of Alberta. He was appointed King's Counsel and, as a corporate, civil, and criminal lawyer, was senior partner in the legal firm of Short, Ross, and Selwood.

In 1938 Central was renamed James Short School, a name it bore for thirty-eight years until it was demolished in 1969. Surviving is the cupola. When the James Short School was razed the suddenly homeless ornament was hauled off to a city storage site near St. George's Island. There it languished on its side, lashed by

Central School, Calgary

This photo shows the old Central School (right), which opened in 1887. Its sandstone successor opened in 1905, next door to the original wooden school. The upper floor was used as a Normal School for instructing teachers. James Short, teacher and lawyer, was the first principal of the new school. In 1938 Central School (the original had been demolished) was renamed James Short School. Though it, in turn, fell to the wrecking ball in 1969, its cupola survived and can be found today in the park located on the site. Courtesy Glenbow-Alberta Institute/NA–1009–5

weather for four years until it was spotted by Calgary oilman J. Richard Harris. He and other Calgarians, including the enthusiastic Local Council of Women, needled the city relentlessly to rescue the artifact from complete deterioration.

More than that, Harris sent letters world-wide in quest of a manufacturer capable of producing a faultless timekeeping mechanism that would complete the decor of the cupola, should it be restored, in the manner envisaged by its designer of so many years ago.

The public donated $1,000 to the project, and Richard Harris, as a gesture of affection for his adopted city, donated $10,000 towards the cost of having the cupola refurbished, transported, and placed on a pedestal on Prince's Island, not far from its original home. It was officially installed on Dominion Day, 1 July 1974, with considerable ceremony and fanfare.

In May 1986 the last piece of the site of the old school was sold. Now the venerable cupola has been moved again, this time to the piece of land upon which it first reached for the sky atop the second Central School.

The Calgary Parks Foundation has elicited many corporate donations and the city has backed creation and maintenance of our newest park. One of the organizations that has added its support for this memorial to our past is our local chamber of commerce. As a commemorative gesture in its centennial year of 1991 that organization created and maintained, in perpetuity, the Calgary Chamber of Commerce Centennial Gardens, a floral centrepiece for the new James Short Park in the presence of those towering buildings that now stand in the heart of our busy city where, just over a century ago, it was no more than a pioneer settler's pasture.

Fond Memories of "the Dog"

*D*uring a recent holiday season an unpredictable and unavoidable combination of severely cold weather, the absence of rail service, the cost of air transportation, and the public's need to travel during the festive season placed intercity travel by bus in a very awkward position. One news reporter wrote:

> Greyhound Lines was scrambling again for extra drivers Wednesday . . . the company hired several other bus companies and drivers to help handle the onslaught of travellers. At least one of the Edmonton drivers was so unfamiliar with the assignment, that he needed his passengers' help to find the new Greyhound terminal here, said one traveller.

It brought to mind a situation told to me in a reminiscent mood about six years ago by the late H.K. "Pat" Williams. He recollected that a man named Gerry Brown was traffic manager for a new Alberta transportation company called Greyhound back in the Dirty Thirties. Williams, who was a railway bridge engineer by profession, was unemployed at the time due to the slump.

Brown, a great transportation expert and enthusiast, talked Pat into taking a driver's job with Greyhound. "I have a taxi outside, and there are thirty-five passengers waiting for a bus down at the depot." Pat's protest that he had never even driven a truck, let alone a highway bus, was to no avail.

On the way into town from the North Hill the taxi driver showed Pat Williams how to double-clutch and change gears without undue noise or effort. Pat said, "He even let me drive a few blocks in order to practise on the way to the Greyhound garage on Eleventh Avenue near Seventh Street West. I wound up paying the cabbie triple fare for his help!"

Pat was given one more fast lesson. One of Greyhound's local owners, Harold "Speed" Olson, took Pat for a quick driving lesson up and down the North Hill on Tenth Street West, declared the rookie ready for the job, then drove him to the depot in the old Herald Building at First Street and Seventh Avenue West where the busload of passengers had been waiting with growing impatience.

Pat recalled that the bus looked huge. He also could still hear Olson commanding him, "Take her to Lethbridge!" As though the delay had not already been enough, before setting out Pat had to collect the tickets from the disgruntled group. The travellers held excursion, one-way, round-trip, and even interline fares. Pat remembered, "I started collecting from the back to the front of the bus. I didn't dare make too big a deal of it because those thirty-five passengers, who had been waiting in the stuffy bus for two hours, were inclined to appear a bit hostile!"

Williams had to assure himself he now was a fully fledged Greyhound bus driver, having received the approval and endorsement of the line's superintendent and part-owner. But, having recently moved to Calgary from Edmonton, he had no idea how to get out of town, heading for Lethbridge!

> A Lethbridge-bound passenger sitting right behind me seemed to be well aware of my problem. So, without being prompted, he began giving me directions: "turn left here," and "take the next right at the intersection up ahead." Soon we were out on the Macleod Trail heading south out of the city.

Happily for me the fellow had made the trip many times so he kept helping me by warning me of the stops up ahead, and pointing out the location of the small-town depots where we had to stop to drop off and pick up passengers and parcels.

It was a good fast bus in top mechanical shape so, with the assistance of the helpful "co-pilot" passenger, and with Pat's learning-while-driving in the matter of double-clutching and road handling, the trip was completed thirty minutes short of the normal travelling time!

Williams became a regular Greyhound driver during the rest of that winter and spring of 1933/34. It turned out to be a very lucky move for Pat. Without knowing it at the time, he had begun a steady climb up through the local Greyhound ranks. At the request of the company's Canadian manager, G.B. Fay, Pat was taken off the roster of drivers and his engineering training was put to work designing an all-steel bus body.

There had been a nasty accident south of Okotoks when a city-bound bus, enveloped in a cloud of traffic dust, had ploughed into a large truck stalled on the highway. The truck's long load of oilwell drill pipe had speared some travellers in the wood-body bus, a fatal tragedy that made it imperative to increase the safety of the Greyhound company's passenger-carriers.

Williams's list of accomplishments for the bus company included designing and supervising the building of forty-five garages and depots in various prairie points. His career moves elevated him to the post of assistant to the president, a position he held until he retired in 1973.

On Tuesday, 14 January 1930, Canadian Greyhound Coaches Limited was created, with headquarters in Calgary. Our city's population stood at about eighty thousand, and all main roads leading to anywhere were narrow, rutted, gravelled, dusty, and riddled with loose stones and potholes.

Automobile registrations in Alberta had not yet reached one hundred thousand and, with the Depression bearing down on everyone, cheap travel was of great importance. In our province the first intercity bus run was from Calgary to Edmonton with Moose Jaw–born Grant Smith at the wheel.

On that initial motor coach run, driver Smith also had the job of recruiting agents in the towns between here and Edmonton who were willing to have their drugstore, confectionery, or whatever, designated as the town's Greyhound depot.

Grant Smith's running time to Edmonton from Calgary that April 1930 took seven bumpy, noisy hours, and he made it without a single passenger! Today on a heavily travelled four-lane highway, the running time between the cities is as fast as three-and-a-half hours.

Opposite: *In January 1930, highway motorbuses of Canadian Greyhound Coaches Limited began fanning out from Calgary to serve passengers in the Pacific northwest between the cities of Edmonton, Spokane, and Vancouver. So-called highways were actually gravelled roads, frequently clogged in winter, and nearly always alarmingly muddy during other seasons. Besides having its headquarters in Calgary, Greyhound (affectionately nicknamed "the Dog") also manufactured its vehicles here. The bus in this 1930 photo was typical. It was an elongated Chevrolet with a Calgary-built, seventeen-passenger body.* Courtesy Glenbow-Alberta Institute/NA–1227–2

Hate or Love
That Municipal Building—
You Can't Ignore It

In 1970 the City of Calgary commissioned two local architects, Raymond Moriyama and Harold Hanen, who designed our city's Plus-30 network, to prepare a plan for a midtown area to include city hall offices, a performing arts centre, and a public open space that would attract Calgarians and visitors to a welcoming and artistic heart of the city.

A November 1979 plebiscite shoved the idea out of the city planners' spotlight. However, an emotional move to restore the white Burns Building on Eighth Avenue East at Second Street revived the idea. Gravely needed expansion of civic office space precipitated the question—to rent or to build?

Again a voter's decision was called for in concert with a civic election of 1980. The electorate chose the building side of the question. Subsequently, at noon 18 October 1985 the City of Calgary officially welcomed a new family member. It is hard to believe that eight years have passed since the Municipal Building was opened.

For me it is a very special city offspring. I had the honour of being named the Calgary-born Senior member of the five-person jury that chose the building design. It was an awesome job, selecting the winning entry and runners-up from the seventy-five competitors in the Alberta-wide architectural contest.

The jury represented widely diverse viewpoints. Professional advisor and jury chairman, who had no vote, was Gustavo da Roza, a Winnipeg architect. The others included Margaret Cadman (now Partridge), a psychology honours graduate of Syracuse University. She stood for the newcomer Calgarians' interests. Joseph Esherick was from San Francisco, chairman of the Architectural Department at the University of California, Berkeley. Fumihiko Maki, a Tokyo architect, had received much of his professional training in the United States, so epitomized the oriental/occidental outlook. Jean Ouillet added his expertise as director of the School of Architecture at the University of Montreal.

All competitors had received an identical briefing of the physical and engineering requirements of the new Municipal Building. When we jurors met for the first time we toured the entire city in a chartered transit bus to give us the sense, layout, and feel of the city to be served by the new building. Then we were sequestered for the balance of the week, a quintet deliberately placed out of business and social touch with the rest of Calgary. Our only contacts with City Hall were Robert Holmes of the city commissioner's office and Frank Byrne, city clerk, both of whom "bird dogged" our personal daily needs during the "squeaky clean" adjudication process.

Each of us on the jury was an opinionated, individualistic specialist in our particular field. The task was to tackle every entry in concentrated and intense detail, assess from our own personal viewpoint the merits and shortcomings of each and, at day's end, summarize, compare, and discuss our findings and opinions.

Some submissions we had to dismiss early in the process because of their agreed-upon inadequacies. We knew each plan

A festive spirit enlivened the little city of forty-four thousand when, in 1911, Calgarians attended the official opening of their new City Hall. The dignified sandstone "head office" was acclaimed as the most modern city hall in the Dominion of Canada, and today it retains its venerable dignity. Alongside it, in significant contrast, stands the Municipal Building, which opened in 1985 and is often referred to as "the New City Hall." Its design, chosen by an international jury, receives some criticism, but for the most part it is admired as a symbol of the dynamism of the city of Calgary. Photo: Bilodeau Preston Limited, Courtesy City of Calgary Commissioner's Office

had to make provision for x number of office employees under climate-controlled conditions; to provide for a dignified and thoroughly workable council chamber; to contain automobile parking and provision for a future underground transit station.

The new building had to have catering facilities; an entryway of quiet distinction; elevator service adequate to the extreme demands of internal office and visiting public foot traffic. Very essential was the need for the new building to present some sort of relationship to the elderly sandstone City Hall.

The structure had to be visible down the Stephen Avenue Mall, yet provide a sophisticated eastward facade that could not be identified as "the back of the building." Those and scores of other specifications had to be considered by the competing architects and the jury members.

We spent silent hours intently studying the anonymous designs' detailing, traffic flows, the practicalities and the aesthetics. I cannot help regarding it, on each of the frequent occasions I do business there, as "my house." From the start I strongly favoured the design that won the Calgary Municipal Building contest.

I hold great sentiment for the City Hall which has been there all my life; and I envisioned the Municipal Building as making a boldly assertive and outspoken contrasting statement as Calgary's business head office.

This $68-million, wedge-shaped glass building on its three-acre site will always have its critics. But it is no re-creation of a domestic or foreign edifice. It is not a gimmicky imitation mimic of history. It is a place to do business and, when one considers the quality of its nearby neighbours that also have arisen in that part of our city, "my house" is here to stay among an increasing array of friends and admirers.

Iron Men of the Foothills

Mr. Henry Wadsworth Longfellow, in the mid-1800s, could not have been aware of the scenic charm of little downtown Calgary when he located his brawny-armed village smithy standing mightily under a spreading chestnut tree.

The fact was, our village's original blacksmith, David Suitor, if ever he had the time to stand around, did so on the bald-headed prairie property occupied by the mounted police compound of Fort Calgary, where he was resident blacksmith.

Having worked also on Colonel Walker's ranch near Cochrane, then at the Walker lumber mill in east Calgary, Suitor opened his own smithy on what was to become Eighth Avenue East. It was a smart move. In those days there were more horses in need of shoes than there were residents in the little settlement.

By 1906 Suitor had opened expanded premises at 410 Atlantic (Ninth) Avenue East where he and his iron-working crew turned out hydrants and water valves for Calgary's fire and engineering departments, streetlamp standards, smoke stacks, pile-driver columns, and decorative ironwork for buildings.

David Suitor prospered. Soon he had a staff of thirty-six and, with the financial help of local lumber barons Peter Prince and Isaac Kerr, and lawyer William McLaws, his firm was established as the Calgary Iron Works. One of the firm's most visible local creations was the decorative wrought iron tower that rose from the rooftop of Balmoral School on the north hill.

One of Suitor's competitors in the early years of this century was William G. Turner, who along with his brother opened a blacksmith shop on Stephen Avenue, where the Queen's Hotel was erected some years later. The Turners also specialized in wrought iron work and, of course, the smithy's standby of those days, the shoeing of farm horses and heavy dray horses as well as the wheelwright skills of fashioning iron tires for wooden wagon wheels and the seasonal job of sharpening ploughshares.

As the years passed, along came other large blacksmith and foundry establishments. The development of wrought iron resulted in the abandonment of a good deal of cast iron, which had a tendency to crack too readily, especially in the bitter cold of Calgary area winters.

A large foundry was part of the CPR's Ogden Shops, where locomotive and other rolling stock repairs were undertaken. Metalworking equipment there included about six overhead rolling cranes with capacities up to 120 tons, and the foundry shop at Ogden produced locally designed and built equipment.

Riverside Iron Works, established by Frederick Lorne Irving and his partner, G.A. Smith, at first occupied land near the Langevin Bridge on the north bank of the Bow River. In later years Riverside's one-time head steel moulder, William Nagel, joined the foundry crew of Dominion Bridge in Calgary's Burnsland district when that sprawling factory turned out six-inch and eight-inch gun barrels during World War II.

Many years earlier, when Calgary was preparing to emerge as a city rather than a frontier town, Atlantic Avenue hotels and blacksmith shops were logical side-by-side neighbours. W.D. Thornton was the blacksmith whose clanging hammer blows rang across the avenue where the Hotel Palliser stands today. Where the

Hotel-Convention Centre/Glenbow Museum Complex occupies a city block, a noisy occupant of part of the site was blacksmith W.H. Lee. One of his neighbours on the block, a few doors to the east on Atlantic, was W.D. Thompson, who did a flourishing business shoeing horses and repairing and replacing carriage-wheel tires. With the popularity of so many firms that hauled every conceivable load—from furniture to milk and bread, and merchandise to travellers' trunks and luggage—the blacksmith shops worked alongside, or inside, the many stables, barns, and wagon storage sheds that peppered early Calgary in pre-automobile days.

My own skimpy connection with that sort of activity took place during the Depression. Under the stern china-blue-eyed gaze of my very practical-minded father I was shanghaied to People's Welding situated right at the brink of the Bow at the foot of First Street East. In order to keep me out of mischief during the otherwise indolent summer holidays from high school in 1931, I grubbed on the oily dirt floor of the dingy little shop.

People's had cornered the oxyacetylene- and electro-welding business of Freeman Motors, Calgary's lone dealer of Hudson and Essex automobiles. I don't know whether it was the fault of the dreadful roads of those days, or a manufacturing weakness of these two lines of passenger cars, but their frames had a tendency to crack just to the rear of the front doors.

So I spent those summer months on my back in a shower of sparks, squeezed under a succession of Essex and Hudson sedans. The homely square-cut Essex was the smaller of the two makes, but even the almost snooty-looking Hudson offered shallow clearance for a small filthy young fellow. However, I learned the perils and the triumph of successfully heating the cracked metal red hot, then melting a metal bead onto and into the flaw.

As daily I wearily made my way home by streetcar and on foot, black as a chimney sweep, and twice as oily, I was shunned by many of my carefree Elbow Park peers. They frolicked rather aimlessly while I, in my dirty coveralls, acquired blackened hands that had to be scrubbed with "Snap" before I could join my friends for evening socializing. I remember being enormously vexed by my father's implacable insistence that I should learn to earn by my hands, rather than by my wits—it was a "bug" of his. But now, very much later in life, I look back with appreciation. I could never earn a living as a blacksmith or welder, but that grimy summer helped teach me discipline and usefulness and the rewards of achieving that Eldorado of youth—earning substantial pocket money!

Opposite: *The Wetmore and Fullerton Blacksmith Shop was one of a great many in the heart of young Calgary. The owners even did some carriage building. Some smithies survived the horse-and-buggy years and kept in business by repairing automobile parts such as frames and axles. Jake Fullerton, seen here with the sledge hammer, was a member of the large and famous Bragg Creek Fullerton ranching family. The shop, like many others, adjoined a hotel, whose guests, in those days, were among every blacksmith's best customers.* Courtesy Glenbow-Alberta Institute/NA–265–7

Our Royal Crown Was Not Diamonds But Soapsuds

*E*vangelist John Wesley preached, in the 1700s, that "Cleanliness is, indeed, next to Godliness." However, two centuries earlier English essayist Francis Bacon had declared that "Cleanliness of body was never deemed to proceed from a due reverence to God." This divergence of opinion may have caused some confusion among church goers but, thank goodness, the cleanliness stance obviously triumphed as an important part of the commerce of early Calgary.

That is because, in 1905, a group of enterprising Calgary businessmen pooled their resources to establish a soap factory in the city of fifteen thousand. As a site they chose some land in the heart of the small manufacturing district with such neighbours as the Calgary Brewery, Hay and Harding's auto body plant, Western Flour's Purity mill and, not too far to the south, one of their big suppliers, Burns and Company's abattoir.

They built a three-storey brick factory on their two-acre plot that was served by a railway spur emerging from the CPR's Alyth yards and that, in 1912, stood directly across the road from Maharg station, the first train stop east of the midtown Calgary depot.

Beginning in 1908, in its first three operational years the soap-making enterprise did very well, yet its backers were not reluctant to accept a buy-out offer from Royal Crown Soaps, which already was making a range of soap products in Winnipeg and Vancouver.

As part of the takeover Royal Crown sent George Nixon Bull, whose father had founded the Winnipeg-headquartered company in the 1890s, to become the new Calgary manager. George, a graduate of Upper Canada College, and thoroughly versed in all aspects of soap making and marketing, was known as a hustling, modern-thinking young executive. He soon had the Calgary plant bursting at the seams with new business.

The staff included forty factory workers, three travelling salesmen, and a teamster with a company wagon and its draft horse team. The firm advertised its territory, shoehorned between its Winnipeg and Vancouver sales territories, as extending "from Moose Jaw to Revelstoke and the Kootenay Landing to the town of Lloydminster . . . truly a wonderful field and one pregnant with possibilities."

Of manager George Bull—remember he was a son of the founder—the firm's florid publicity stated that "from the first day in which he took over the work, the business of the Royal Crown Soap Company has grown and increased until today it stands without rival in the western world largely, if not altogether, owing to the hard work of the man entrusted with the management of the concern."

Sixty years ago the people who dreamed up the company's advertising were in love with their own words, for this was their pitch: "Royal Crown Soap is essentially a local product since all the tallows, as well as other raw materials that can be produced in Alberta, are purchased here . . . Most of the vegetable oils have to be purchased abroad, Coconut Oil coming from the Philippines (misspelled Phillipines in the ad!), Soy Bean Oil from Manchuria, and Olive Oil from Italy. Practically all other materials are

Royal Crown Soap, made in Calgary by the only soap works on the Prairies, travelled the world. It was used on every CPR train, in all the CPR line's hotels, and aboard every CP coastal and ocean-going steamship. This sketch of the factory that made Golden West and Royal Crown soaps appeared on a street map published about 1910 by The Calgary Daily Herald. Courtesy Glenbow-Alberta Institute/NA–3681–12

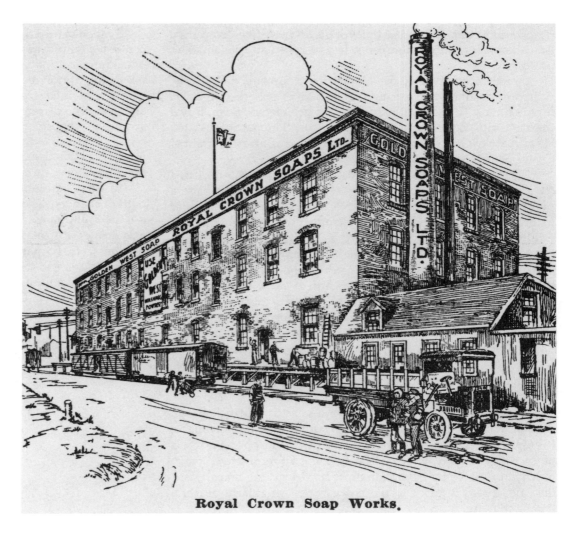

Royal Crown Soap Works.

purchased in Canada, and as the work is all performed by purely Canadian labor, the product can safely be called an All-Canadian product."

If one were to believe the advertising trumpeted in 1923, the company products were truly legion and as progressive as its management. Their brand names were Pure Electric Soap, Royal Electric Chips, Concentrated Lye Soap, Water Softener Soap, Witch Hazel, Crown Olive (a special vegetable oil soap), an assortment of Castile Soap, and Bath Soap.

"The main laundry soap, Royal Crown Soap, is manufactured on a special formula for use in Western waters which have a peculiar hardness, account of which is taken in the process of manufacture. It is truly a Western Product for Western People," wrote the hucksters.

Then there came a turning point in the company's history. The potential of George Nixon Bull, the soap tycoon, was recognized by the big Liverpool-based English soap firm of Lever Brothers. That international organization bought the Calgary plant and Bull, now an employee of Lord Leverhulme, was promoted and transferred to the new owner's Toronto offices. Taking over the reins here was Toronto-born David G. Sturrock. He found himself in charge of seventy-five employees operating a factory with nine soap kettles and a manufacturing appetite for tallows and greases produced by packing houses throughout Alberta.

One of George Bull's innovations inherited by Sturrock was an in-plant staff dining room at which a generous menu was available to employees at cost. The company took care of the operating costs of the dining facility, which, in its day, was an innovative "perk" much appreciated by the staff in those hard-working times. Possibly, too, it was a factor in the soap works' singularly peaceful labour climate.

Sixteen-year-old Eva Jagoe was one of those hard-working, contented employees. She wanted to become a schoolteacher, and one summer a job as a soap packer helped her accumulate her university tuition fees. She told me, "I didn't use the dining room because we lived close enough to the factory for me to have lunch at home. But I do remember the endless stream of bars and bars of soap that we girls, on either side of a moving belt, packed into boxes." She also remembered the girls standing almost knee-deep in bars of soft new soap. The supervisor refused to stop the production line just because, he said, the girls worked too slowly!

In time the entire marketing and the raw material source pattern changed. There was no more mixing of oils from Manchuria, the Philippines, and Italy. Lever Brothers no longer felt there was a sales advantage in catering to our local water's "peculiar hardness," for so many years a key ingredient of the sales pitch. So Calgary's east end soap-making plant closed its doors for good.

So ended a very unusual Calgary manufacturing story. In its heyday local Royal Crown Soaps Limited products were known worldwide. The Canadian Pacific Railway's slogan was "Spans the World." On all the company's trans-Atlantic and trans-Pacific liners, on its trains and in all its hotels, could be found Royal Crown advertising that said, "Witch Hazel, a high class toilet soap . . . that is used by the C.P.R. from Liverpool to Hong Kong."

Vittles for Cowpokes and City Slickers

*F*or lonely bachelors who came here to "make a fortune" before sending for their families to join them out on the western frontier, many meals at Calgary's original boarding houses and hotels were not familiar home-cooking, but they were substantial.

One "married but single" pioneer, general store merchant Isaac S. Freeze, a native of Penobsquis, New Brunswick, was a prolific writer of diarylike letters to his wife back home. In one letter written in December 1883, right after his first Christmas away from his wife and children, was the brief yet poignant comment, "I have spent a very dull Christmas but had a good dinner at the Royal Hotel."

One had to be content with the simplest of facilities in those days. The Royal Hotel opened in August 1883 as a pair of large tents, one for sleeping, one for the cooking and dining. Before winter set in, a wooden structure, said to have been hauled by rail from Regina, replaced the tents.

During the early years of Calgary's existence prior to 1900, hotels were not the only caterers, although Calgary's first restaurant appears to have been located in the Alberta House Hotel. It was owned and operated by L.S. Johnson before being sold to S.J. Clark, an ex-mountie who also became an alderman on Calgary's original city council. Boarding houses, most of which were on Stephen and Atlantic (Eighth and Ninth) avenues, close to the railway station, of course supplied meals for their own residents. The Mountain View Hotel was one such Atlantic Avenue establishment in 1884. It claimed to serve meals for "respectable day boarders."

One of its neighbours on Atlantic Avenue across from the station was the Woodbine Dining Hall and Saloon. Nearby were the Gerald House and the Virginia Chop House. Many years later, at the end of the Great War, the CPR Lunch Counter was situated within the station itself. It backed onto the ticket counter on the west side of the main rotunda and was a very clean stopping-place for colonist-car and day-coach rail travellers.

During the twenty-minute Calgary halt, passengers were lured by the good low-cost meals and swift service in the noisy white-tiled restaurant. Upon the arrival of each long-distance train a lunch-counter employee wearing a white bib apron emerged onto the trackside platform and rang a large hand-bell to alert new arrivals of food service. The CPR Lunch Counter's reputation for excellent and varied meals at popular prices extended to Calgary's downtown business community, whose professionals and merchants were soon loyal patrons.

With similar "decor"—acoustically harsh, but with gleaming white tiles, high ceiling, bare marble-topped tables, and fast good food—were the White Lunch cafes. One was on Eighth Avenue West, the other fairly near the CPR station on Ninth. They were cafeterias, urging Calgarians to "Try eating here—all the substantials—all the dainties—prices that will suit you."

According to the research of Calgary historian William M. McLennan (in his book *Bed and Breakfast: A History of Hostelries and Eating Establishments in the Area of Calgary*, 1989) there were wild fluctuations in the number of Calgary's eating places due to our community's "boom and bust" lifestyle, the dwindling number of male customers due to overseas wars, and the erosion of the economy during the Great Depression of the 1930s. For example, in 1913 Calgary had seventy-nine eating places of which eighteen were on Eighth Avenue. Yet by 1918, in addition to hotel cafes, we had only forty-six restaurants, and by 1945 we were back up to sixty-one.

Throughout the years citizens who "ate out" locally had no shortage of food choices ranging from the 1800s when wildfowl and buffalo tongue and hump were standard fare, to turn-of-the-century imported seasonal delicacies from as far afield as Europe. As McLennan discovered, "At various times during the year local restaurants served such varied seafood as Utah lake bass, catfish, mountain trout, striped bass, Hamburg eels, shad, and prawns. Calgary restaurants offered squab, grouse, mallard, teal, plover, pheasant, quail or partridge. Oysters were a favorite . . . "

Of course, throughout the early years Chinese food was available in such Calgary establishments as Wing Fong's, Shanghai Chop Suey, the Hong Kong, W.K. Chop Suey, Charlie Kee's, Kwong Man Yuen, Sun Chun Wah, and the Mandarin Gardens. In fact, in earlier days, of our little city's twenty-seven cafes, a dozen were Chinese owned and operated.

Looking back, it seems that young Calgary was basically pretty much of a "meat and potatoes" town when agriculture and livestock were our chief sources of livelihood. Generous helpings of nourishing, if unimaginative, food were the stock-in-trade of most eating spots. Beef ribs, loin of pork, macaroni and cheese, steamed puddings, and raisin pie could be found wherever the ketchup and coffee pot roamed. One noticeable ethnic holdover was the busy existence of half a dozen "Old Country" fish and chip shops.

Starting in the mid 1960s, the discovery of huge oil deposits spawned the invasion of oil families from the United States, many of whom had a background of world-wide living. They notably influenced our eating habits and our diets. We learned about tollhouse, praline, pizza, lasagna, gazpacho, sushi, sukiyaki, quiche, pasta, guacamole—new words, aromas, ideas, and tastes in our kitchens and in our vocabularies as our taste buds became cosmopolitan. Surely, however, this is an imported Americanism that defies a gourmet's logic: Chinese Smorgasbord!

Opposite: *Although in its younger days Calgary was regarded as having a "meat and potatoes" frontier-type appetite, there were many restaurants. One was the Plaza, with a tiny dance floor, a three-piece band, and long tablecloths, under which one could hide a liquor bottle during prohibition days.* Courtesy Glenbow-Alberta Institute/NA–1469–15

Silver Rail Shuttles Knit Alberta

In 1956, Albertans came face-to-face with a revolution in rail travel. The Rail Diesel Cars, RDCs, we came to know as the CN Railiner and the CP Dayliner, like bright silver shuttles, began weaving up, down, and across our province.

The RDCs were not the first self-propelled rail cars to appear here. As long ago as 1925 Canadian National Railways had sent forth North America's first diesel-electric car, a Canadian invention, to cross much of our country on a test run. The revolutionary unit accomplished the 2,930-mile Montreal-Vancouver trip in five minutes short of fifty-seven hours, much to the astonishment of all who watched the unusual vehicle race by. The imaginative Canadian builders could only hope their self-contained, diesel-powered, electrically driven brainchild would find an important place in our national transportation pattern.

An offshoot of the Canadian invention was the U.S.-built Budd RDC that came in four 550-horsepower models. All were put to work in Alberta by the western divisions of both main railways. One model, twenty-eight-and-a-half yards in length, had a carrying capacity of ninety passengers. Another had seating for seventy and room for about five tons of freight. Still another had a divided capacity for forty-eight passengers and over six tons, and the fourth model, about twenty-five yards long, was a fifteen-ton express and freight carrier.

Eagerly placed in service by the Canadian Pacific and the Canadian National systems, the RDCs slashed running times between Alberta centres. Their metallic fluted sides, garish diagonal end striping, reciprocating headlights, and bleating horns became less and less of a novelty as they proved their worth. Although they cost about twice the price of a steam engine, the running costs were being reduced to about 80¢ per mile from about $3 per mile for a conventional steam-powered passenger train.

The first Alberta use of the RDCs was on the Canadian Pacific Calgary-Edmonton line. A combination of motorists' respect for the new rocketing cars and lighter road traffic made the rail journey in those days swift and reliable. The intercity run took three-and-a-half hours, a two-hour saving over the old steam engine trip. Before long the CP Dayliner service was augmented by links between Calgary and Lethbridge, Calgary and Moose Jaw, and Lethbridge and Medicine Hat. An hour-and-a-half travelling time was cut from the Calgary-Lethbridge run, the twice-daily service taking only two hours and forty minutes.

Until the Canadian Pacific abandoned passenger service on its southern trans-mountain line, Dayliners shuttled between Lethbridge and Vancouver on our nation's truly spectacular daytime route. An advertisement extolled the scenic advantages of leaving the mainliner "Canadian" at Medicine Hat and taking the westbound rail car at 10:20 each morning. It urged: "Enjoy travel aboard these new stainless steel rail diesel cars with reclining seats."

Lethbridge was reached at noon, Cranbrook at 5:35, and Nelson at 10:15, allowing passengers to enjoy a night's sleep in a Nelson hotel. They set off westward at 7:00 in the morning, arriving

Introduced to Alberta in 1956, Rail Diesel Cars (RDC) were named Dayliners by the CPR and Railiners by the CNR. In one- and two-car units, these high-speed vehicles replaced steam-powered trains, carrying passengers and express. They noticeably shortened running times between Calgary and Edmonton, Calgary and Lethbridge, and on sections of east-west Alberta routes. These diesel-electrics were descendants of the world's first mainline diesel, pioneered in 1925 in Canada by the CNR. Courtesy Canadian Pacific/M 6655

at Hope at 9:00 P.M., ready for a speedy run in the gathering dark down the Fraser Valley to arrive in Vancouver at 11:20.

The eastbound trip, with an early morning Vancouver departure, allowed unhurried travellers an afternoon and overnight stay in Penticton, then a daylight trip to another night in Nelson! The leg east from Nelson through mountains, foothills, and prairie ended either with a prompt Dayliner connection to Calgary, or eastward to Medicine Hat to join the eastbound mainline train at 8:20 P.M.

There was a footnote to the advertisement: "'Dayliner' service will be extended between Nelson and Penticton as soon as additional rail diesel cars are delivered." New units did arrive, yet the Calgary-Lethbridge Dayliner run was shut down on 3 July 1971, marking the end of another chapter in our province's rail passenger story.

Canadian National kept its Dayliners on the move for twenty-one years while various models of RDCs raced across the Canadian scene between Nova Scotia's Annapolis Valley and British Columbia's Pacific shore. The last of CN's Calgary-based passenger rail diesel cars pulled out of the old sandstone station on First Street West on 17 April 1979.

But well before that Canadian National, with a twice-daily Railiner running between Calgary and Edmonton via Camrose, and between Drumheller and Edmonton via Stettler, chalked up some innovative time-saving runs. In 1958 it added a fast "merchandise only" service to its passenger and express traffic. Replacing a twice-weekly steam way-freight, the Railiners created a one-of-a-kind service between Calgary and Edmonton. They made the daily 232-mile run in five-and-a-half hours, including thirty-two stops to unload and pick up cargo. Crated animals, auto accessories, cartons of chicks, implement parts, mail-order furniture, farm produce, "anything we can get through the express car door" became cargo for the Railiners along a merchandise lifeline of fifteen manned, and seventeen unmanned, express points. Irricana, Trochu, Three Hills, Elnora, and Mirror were some of the brief and busy pauses in the Railiners' race with time on this unique nonpassenger service.

But not only had the glamour of steam trains vanished, now the economic appeal of the RDCs was fast diminishing. Interurban highway trucking gained the upper hand, even though rail travel was still favoured by many because of its all-weather reliability.

I had an opportunity to ride at the front of a northbound Dayliner one winter morning many years ago when a blizzard had forced all other transportation to a halt. Standing close behind the engineer's shoulder I found it an astonishing experience as the Dayliner, its speedometer needle unwavering at the approved speed limit, hurled itself at the white wall of the storm. At times the tracks were completely obliterated by drifting snow but the throbbing machine, almost as though hurtling across open fields, thrust its way through the snow spume to arrive in Edmonton on time.

The now-controversial offspring of that early Canadian creation of 1925 are gone from our local scene. But during their short lifespan they were responsible for very fast, reliable passenger and express services across Alberta, as they still are in a few parts of our nation.

If They Flattened It Out, It Would Just Be Prairie

Calgarians who have not lived here very long are inclined to regard as pretty corny our local western habit of giving highways and expressways the name of Trail—for example, Crowchild, Deerfoot, Barlow, and Macleod. These names are constant reminders to our wheeled population that our past is not too far behind us!

Only about three generations ago Memorial Drive was an extension of the original Blackfoot Indian trail leading from the Gleichen area to the mountains. Maps may still be found with Richmond Road wearing its original name of the South Morley Trail. Within the city were routes that were unmistakably named for their direction, destination, or purpose.

A road once called the Magazine Trail angles off to the southwest from the first bench of the Fourteenth Street SW hill that today leads to South Calgary. That upwardly sloped road trailed rather informally past the southern edge of the Oliver sandstone quarry and headed out towards South Morley Trail. The hill-climbing part, now numbered Nineteenth Avenue, ambles up through Bankview, and now takes a distinct left turn to become Richmond Road. Once upon a time, when that was original prairie, it led to a cave hollowed in the hillside, well removed from habitation, in which explosives were stored for the mounted police and the Town of Calgary, hence the name Magazine Trail.

We lost many colourful street names when, in 1904, the City of Calgary gave pioneer surveyor A.P. Patrick the job of laying the midtown area in an unyielding grid pattern and giving the streets and avenues numbers instead of the names they had borne since the railway station was established west of the Elbow River. Two, in particular, have had their names restored: Stephen and Barclay.

Some of our streets' and avenues' names have lived on, although they lost their original identities in the numbers game of 1904. Pioneer west-end rancher Billy Nimmons watched the little city creeping towards his imposing brick mansion on the first bench of the Fourteenth Street West hill. He sensed doom for the names of the roads he had anticipated for the district now known as the Beltline. He had given them the names of his children—William, George, Kate, and Isabella. Sure enough, they became numbers, although in the new residential areas of Scarboro and Mount Royal, somebody's hard-headed persistence paid off. The stubborn insistence on names as opposed to numbers probably could be laid at the doorstep of the original landowner, the Canadian Pacific Railway.

In much more recent years, newly created thoroughfares have been given trail names such as Peigan, Bow Bottom, and Marquis of Lorne. Additionally there are historic names such as Brisebois Drive, remembering the upstart young mountie who named the police fort after himself before his knuckles were rapped by his superior officers for his arrogance.

There is John Laurie (not Laurier) Boulevard named after a quiet and dedicated gentleman school teacher and champion of Indians in these parts. Gone is Strawberry Hill, now known as Pump Hill. Gone is the once flat prairie area of Moccasin Flats, now overrun by parts of Victoria Park and Mission. Of course when the

On an early springtime land inspection trip in the Bowness area, five city officials, in a 1912 Haynes touring car, grind up a hill above the Bow River. Swift mountain-born rivers have carved deep valleys in the Calgary area, which, along with the foothills, make for anything but flat prairie land, although Calgary is known as a prairie city. Courtesy Glenbow-Alberta Institute/NA–3429–1

land developers took over, nearly all the old names were not good enough. Erased from the maps were Kitsilano, the Rhubarb Patch, Winona Heights, Little Rosevale, Hiawatha, Beaumont, the Bronx and Golden Bronx, Brewery Flats, University Plateau, Manitou Park, Avondale, Highgate, and Chesterfield.

Onto the Calgary scene have emerged such ill-fitting names as Diamond Cove, Sienna Hills, Catalina, Monterey, and the Orchards; no less odd, I admit, than that of the once bald-headed Forest Lawn!

Street naming, in my opinion, reached absurd heights when the city and developers, obsessed with an idea, went to the greatest possible lengths to match thoroughfare names to those of their new residential areas. One committee was struck to find snug, smug "U" names for University Heights, which was about to be developed.

One wag suggested a street should be named Ungracious for home purchasers who planned to surround their property with high board fences. Uncanny would suit Scottish-born buyers, and Usurper would recognize non-Calgarians! Uvula was suggested for doctors buying new homes close to Foothills Hospital. A circular street without ending, it was proposed, would constitute the heavily mortgaged area's commercial addresses of bankers and other money-lending firms. It would be christened Usury Drive!

Some years later similarly pixilated minds generated some really warped names to fit the "Lake" pattern. Thus Emerald Lake, for instance, became Lake Emerald and Waterton had its age-old title reversed as Lake Waterton—anything to make the crime fit the punishment!

The aesthetic sensibilities of home-owners always appear to be soothed by a named address, rather than a numbered one. Also, the habit of using a name common to all thoroughfares in a specific residential area is of help to emergency services such as fire, police,

and ambulance. The practice, though, almost painted itself into a corner until a family of adjectival appendages was created.

Hence today we live with such addresses as Cinnamon Hill, Cinnamon Close, Crescent, Bay, Grove, Mews, Drive—everything but Cinnamon Bun. I don't suppose it is possible to run out of names destined to serve the magic of the home-buyers' imaginations. That subdivision master developer, the late E.V. Keith, instead of using the names of the original landowners George Manitaws and Wilfred Rivers chose, instead, the much more marketable name of Willow Park.

Some vintage-named thoroughfares may occupy maverick status amid those sharing a district's Christian name or surname. Purposefully titled in commemoration of Calgarians' occupations are Gissing Drive (artist), Burns Avenue (beef), Lindsay Drive (medicine), Samis Road (administration), Simons Valley Road (ranching), Rundle Crescent (religion), Cartier Street (exploring), and College Lane (having been a boundary of today's high school's predecessor, Western Canada College).

Let's hope the Turner Valley oil discoverer's name does not tickle some area-namers' fancies. I can see it now—the new subdivision of Dingman bearing the names Dingbat Crescent, Ding-a-Ling Close, Dingledangle Drive, and Ding-Dong Dell, (or should that be Avon Lady Lane?).

Victoria—The Stampede's Long-suffering Neighbour

Calgary's historic community of Victoria is very much in the news these days. Whatever its boundaries were in past years, I am told it now is edged by the "L" of the Elbow River on the south and east, by Tenth Avenue along the north, and First Street East on the west. To look at it today is to see acres of levelled empty space because much of the old residential area has been bought and demolished for such uses as car parking for the Stampede.

The spotlight of the Victoria neighbourhood love-hate relationship always focuses upon the Stampede's voracious high-profile July appetite for elbow room. Its vocal neighbours still fear that that institution's many other tasty events held throughout the rest of the year may constitute stealthy snacks that could gobble the rest of what once was a distinctive part of the core settlement of Calgary.

By the summer of 1889, away off to the south of town, in the crook of the Elbow River, lay about ten acres of prairie that could be purchased for $235. To Colonel James Walker and his fellow members of the Calgary Agricultural Society it seemed an ideal site for the group's annual exhibition, so they bought it.

The venture was far from successful mainly because would-be exhibitors and patrons felt it was much too far out of town. But as time passed, the little city spread southward across the prairie. By 1911 the community of Victoria, neatly built up on streets and avenues, consisted of single-family houses, stores, small factories, and perhaps the most vital component of the area, the new and specially designed sandstone Calgary General Hospital.

The hospital opened its doors in May 1895 on Twelfth Avenue and Sixth Street East with accommodation for thirty-five patients. One of the staff's working headaches was the isolation ward, Calgary's first, that was set up in a very large tent across Twelfth Avenue from the hospital proper. In those days little was known about contagion and infection but, in time, as medical knowledge and skills developed and improved, it was thought to be safe to integrate those patients under the common roof of the hospital.

After the new two-hundred-bed General Hospital was opened in Sunnyside, the old one became the city's first Isolation Hospital. Then, in 1953, it reopened as a senior citizens' home before being demolished to make way for a new Rundle Lodge in 1973. Today, in the form of sandstone ruins, part of the old hospital building is a permanent outdoor memorial park.

Another of Victoria's early large buildings stood closer to the Elbow than the hospital. For a time during and following the Boer War it was used by the militia as a drill hall, especially for the 103rd (Calgary Rifles) Regiment. Next it was utilized as an army equipment depot during World War I while defence authorities in Ottawa dithered for seven years about a permanent site for a Calgary armoury.

When the Mewata location was chosen over Victoria Park the structure was taken over by a baker named J.T. Mitchell (no connection with John W. Mitchell, one of Calgary's mayors) who manufactured "Perfection Bread," which enjoyed considerable city-wide popularity. Although very many years have passed, that

This photo was taken during the first Stampede, which was introduced as an additional attraction to the annual Agricultural Fair at Victoria Park. Historic and legal deeds specified that the park could not be dissected or used for purposes other than a park. The adjoining neighbourhood of Victoria logically inherited the name but, because of the constant urging of the Stampede Board for expanded facilities, Victoria's past is dead, its present shaky, and its future is anybody's guess. Courtesy Glenbow-Alberta Institute/NA–335–60

Fourteenth Avenue and Sixth Street East address is still as aromatic because, for over three-quarters of a century, it was somebody's bakery.

An old timer that has disappeared was our city's steam-driven power station at the river's edge in Victoria Park. Others were the rail yard, car barn, and maintenance workshops of our street railway system. Having begun its life as a passenger carrier between the fairgrounds and the city centre, the Calgary Municipal Railway incongruously settled itself on a fairly narrow strip of city-owned, north-south land bordered by the Macleod Trail, the Elbow River, and the exhibition's acreage.

In the heart of the district is Victoria School, which had a modest beginning in 1903 as a four-room wooden building. Then, in 1919, at the height of Calgary's sandstone school-building splurge, Victoria School was born anew. Now its continued existence is menaced by a forecast shortage of pupils, but its long and illustrious history is well remembered and documented by its alumni.

One of the original school's little-trumpeted claims to fame was that it became the third Calgary schoolhouse to be equipped with a modern heating system and indoor plumbing. For decades that school has been a focal point of many vigorous community endeavours. Despite the demolition of so many of the area's residences and the enormous changes, its community relations seem to be as strongly cemented as ever.

In 1984 Victoria, or Victoria Park as it is more commonly known, was inducted into Calgary's Area Development Program. Even with the sometimes ominous changes in civic growth planning (the intrusion of the Olympic Saddledome, built for the XV Winter Olympic Games, being one of them) this old-time neighbourhood appears to have an admirably tenacious will to live on as one of our more venerable and historic inner city heritages.

When Two Stubborn Objects Meet ...

*I*n 1907 Calgary had forty-one registered automobiles. One of the few people to ride in one was newspaper reporter Earle Young, who was taken for a drive by Calgary lumber tycoon Peter Prince. The vehicle was a Rambler, the first gasoline-powered car in Calgary. After the ride, Young wrote: "Personally I don't think the automobile will ever amount to much, except in a country where there aren't any horses, and then the possibility of frequent breakdowns will make them useless."

Disagreeing with him was *Calgary Herald* editor J.J. Young, who bought an automobile in 1905. It is difficult to determine the view of R.B. Bennett, the lawyer who was to become our prime minister. That same year he bought an Oldsmobile that got the better of him, thus chalking up one of the city's very early auto mishaps. The dignified Bennett mistakenly drove onto the Stephen Avenue sidewalk and allowed his car to butt one of our midtown bank buildings.

Before a year had passed the newspaper was telling a different tale, perhaps due to an outstanding feat of trailblazing that began early on the morning of 3 March 1906. Calgarian H.W. White, who had just taken delivery of a Ford car in Edmonton, undertook to drive his shiny new black "tourer" to Calgary. With him was the young son of the Edmonton car dealer, and a mechanically minded Innisfail man by the name of G.T. Lundy.

The first leg of the trip was through snow but as they approached Lacombe the motorists found the road (such as it was!) clear. White managed to whiz along at the dazzling speed of forty miles per hour. It took them most of two days to complete the trip and they pulled into Calgary, bone-shaken and weary but triumphant, at seven o'clock on the evening of 4 March.

In the summer of 1906 *The Calgary Weekly Herald* opined, "The automobile is in Calgary to stay and its number is increasing every week. The car craze, if it can be called a craze, has only struck Calgary this summer. Until this year people were deterred from purchasing autos owing to the fear that it would be difficult to keep them in order. Now that a garage has been established this fear no longer exists." That garage advertised: "Automobile and typewriter repairs a specialty!" The proprietor must have rejoiced at the prospect of a booming business thanks to the newspaper's romantic enthusiasm.

Someone on staff wrote, "The only thing necessary to convert a motor-hater into a motor-lover is a spin over the smooth roads of the foothill country around Calgary. There is nothing more exhilarating. It is the poetry of motion, the ideal mode of travelling for business or pleasure. From present indications next year will see forty or fifty automobiles in Calgary." Perhaps the faulty arithmetic was due to the excitement created by this new piece of mobile machinery.

However modest that 1906 prediction might have been, by 1912 Calgary had 654 registered automobiles. However, even back then it was clear that a reliable vehicle was not the only requirement to popularize motoring. There still had to be some skill behind the steering wheel.

Fire Chief James "Cappy" Smart was soon to become a victim of just such a circumstance. As chief smoke-eater one of his job perks was a horsehide-upholstered McLaughlin touring car. En route to a fire in the winter of 1912 his vehicle and a streetcar collided at Ninth Avenue and Second Street SE. The smashup was enough to sideline the ex-mortician for almost two years.

In 1909 Julien Chatel opened a garage that was in business for many years. It resembled an old grey barn and was located on Fifth Street and Twelfth Avenue SW. He was a genius at doctoring balky vehicles, including those with experimental electrical gadgets.

That same year F.L. Irving and his brother Ernest, with a third partner, George Hanna, opened their car repair shop under the name of the Central Garage, on Sixth Avenue and Second Street SE. Another well-trained pioneer motor mechanic in Calgary was Antoine A. Jullien. He had learned his trade helping to make costly high-speed automobiles at the Rocket-Schneider plant in France. Beginning in 1911 he was located on Sixteenth Avenue and Ninth Street SW, behind the Devenish Apartments.

Those were the days, despite the newspaper's fantasy of smooth foothills roads, that aggressively tested the metal and the mettle of car and driver. They taxed the ingenuity of those original garagemen, too. Those early internal combustion engines, so simple by today's standards, were mysterious and new and alarmingly temperamental.

I realized how intrepid were those pioneer motorists as I browsed through a 1914 publication entitled the *Official Tour Book of the Alberta Motor Clubs*. It had strip maps that were far from complete, and there was a plaintive preface asking motorists to note their routes and mileages in order to share their findings with other travellers.

The book contained advertisements for Maltese Tires, Thermoid Brake Linings, Warren's Waterless Gasoline, and Sunshine Coal Oil. For cleaning the trim on your car you were urged to try Rei Hei Brand brass polish, or a very clever product of the Quality Oil Company of Calgary: "Our Silver Polish turns brass to silver instantly."

One of the guide's full-page advertisements was inserted by Pryce Jones (Canada) Limited—a pre–Great War, Welsh-based Calgary department store for which the Traders Building, on First Street and Twelfth Avenue SW, was erected. The ad read, "The Motoring Season extends over 12 months of the year. In Alberta we have something appropriate for the auto tourist for any and all seasons: Coats, Gloves, Caps, Gauntlets, Shoes, Furs, Rugs, Leggings." Obviously when it, Calgary, and the century were all very new, motoring indeed was an outdoor sport!

Opposite: *Automobiles and accidents are inseparable. Even when Calgary had a tiny motorcar population there were tangles. This one, in 1912, nearly demolished Fire Chief James "Cappy" Smart, too. The official fire department McLaughlin Buick was no match for a streetcar, and nobody was even going to a fire at the time!* Courtesy Glenbow-Alberta Institute/NA–1615–1

The Palace That Was Not Fit for a King

*I*t is a fairly common occurrence in our city, which has such a telescoped history, to discover a new building replacing an original. In this case a "second generation" structure is slated for oblivion because it is deteriorating at an unpleasant rate. The thirty-year-old multilevel parking building may well be succeeded by a ground-level parking lot because of a long-term commitment to its hotel neighbour across the street. The location is the northwest corner of Centre Street and Ninth Avenue West. Condemned and closed for a year because of its disintegration due to road salt dripping from parked cars, this Calgary Parking Authority structure had been the daily resting place for 423 vehicles.

That midtown quarter-block has a much more colourful history than that of an auto stable. Oddly, part of it was once was a horse stable: the Windsor Hotel Livery and Feed Barn. In 1906 the Centre Street frontage of that corner was occupied by Halse's Cafe, Miller's Barber Shop, the Prince of Wales Cafe and, taking up the whole corner, the Palace Hotel.

On the Ninth Avenue frontage west of the Palace were Daniel's Restaurant, the Windsor Hotel, then its livery stable. Those business premises were razed as time went on. Outlasting the others were the Mandarin Gardens fronting onto Centre Street and the Palace Hotel, which occupied the whole corner itself. Theirs was an ideal location opposite the busy CPR station where much of the pedestrian traffic was made up of immigrants to Calgary.

The Palace Hotel was owned by Charlie Bell, a prodigious drinker of champagne who also owned the Royal Hotel, which stood a block away from the Palace. The main entrance to the two-storey brick veneer building was angled on the street corner and the place looked quite hospitable, especially since it was painted a deceptive white, though unsuspecting guests often had to share their beds with the bugs!

There was a spot of trouble at the "lily white" hotel when the annual Calgary Polo Club banquet of 1895 was held there without a proper Northwest Territories liquor permit. The management was either forgetful or defiant, for, much to its many regular clients' disgust, it again lost its liquor permit in 1902. Loyal tipplers put together and successfully submitted a petition, but soon the Palace Hotel, along with its bar, was closed forever. Its replacement, the Palace Rooms, was hardly any more savoury.

The building of the parking structure sounded the death knell of the Mandarin Gardens, next to the Palace Rooms on Centre Street. One of my long-time correspondents, Jack Welsford of

Opposite: *Most of Calgary's original hotels extended along Atlantic (Ninth) Avenue, bunched as closely as possible facing the CPR station. Varying widely in atmosphere and amenities, they were handy for travellers and offered reasonable rates. The Palace Hotel, a palace in name only, was directly opposite the station's main entrance. Later, as the Palace Rooms, its accommodations were available by the hour, day, or week, but its reputation remained much the same. In this 1912 photo, owner Carl Wieting and his daughter pose with the staff. Courtesy Glenbow-Alberta Institute/NA–4413–4*

Acme, recalled the days when he was a coal-mine shipping clerk in Drumheller Valley. He remembered " . . . arriving in Calgary when the Mandarin nightspot and eatery was off limits to armed forces personnel. I had a crippling bout of flu and a six-hour layover between trains. I talked the 'Mandarin' into letting me have a room at half-price until train time. Now every time I read about them tearing down a building in Calgary they're not tearing down buildings, they're tearing down memories."

The Mandarin held many memories for musician Elmer Peck, who played bass and guitar for a dollar a night during the Depression. He often performed at the Mandarin with Lou Darby and His Hawaiians. They were music makers who were glad to have a chance to make some money playing rather than going on welfare.

One evening during prohibition days (July 1916 to November 1923), Elmer and his musician friends sort of "waddled" into the Mandarin Gardens because each man had a mickey of rye or gin in his hip pocket. Once the quartet was seated, the bottles were parked on the floor near the table legs. In those days, the table-cloths were deliberately long and droopy—as a camouflage measure. The waiter would automatically supply one with glasses and ice and an extra set of tumblers. Out of the corner of his mouth the customer would order bottles of Orange Crush, ginger ale, or Zem Zem mix. Then, when everyone was absolutely sure nobody was looking, weird motions went on under the tablecloth as shots were poured into glasses while the culprits feigned innocence.

Your inane conversation and covert looks would make you feel safe from the gimlet eyes of police who were constantly dropping in, on the prowl for liquor violators. Woe betide any diners they spotted who appeared to stagger onto the small dance floor.

Memories of the Palace Hotel and the Mandarin Gardens night spot—relics of what some people love to misguidedly recall as "the good old days"—will also be buried beneath the asphalt of a parking lot, like so much of Calgary's past.

Nimble-fingered Santa's Elves

*B*ack in the 1920s and 1930s a large and memorable youthful Christmastime event for children of Calgary's many underfunded families was the annual Toy Shop. It was a joint effort of the Boy Scouts and Girl Guides, the Wolf Cubs, Brownies, and Rovers.

Its instigator was F. Leslie Sara, a manufacturers' representative and scoutmaster of the Tenth Troop in Rideau. He hatched the idea while accompanying the manager of a Calgary department store assessing the post-Christmas, pawed-over remnants of the store's toy department. Sara's enthusiasm for a soiled-toy repairing venture was contagious. Lt. Col. J.H. Woods, publisher of *The Calgary Herald*, was putting together the Herald Sunshine Society, which would sponsor food hampers for local needy families. The idea of adding toys to next year's Christmas hampers fit in perfectly with his plan.

The Kiwanis Club picked up the idea, too, and supplied tools, hardware, solder, paint, glue, and plaster of Paris, for every kind of toy repair job. As the winter of 1923 approached the first Toy Shop was organized, housed in the empty former Merchants Bank of Canada building on the southeast corner of Centre Street and Eighth Avenue.

Scores of uniformed young scouts and cubs, as well as guides and brownies manned the workbenches and loaner sewing machines, spending every spare evening and weekend hour refurbishing wind-up toy vehicles, re-wigging dolls, painting, mending, sewing, and rebuilding used playthings.

Each November the Capitol and the Palace movie theatres held a Toy Matinee at which Harold Lloyd, Charlie Chaplin, and Fatty Arbuckle comedy films were shown to packed houses of youngsters. Their admission price was a new toy or one that could be mended.

One of my own vivid Toy Shop memories is of suddenly encountering, on the upper floor of the workplace, an open box of eyes—all staring up at me, each pair vacantly gazing from under obviously false eyelashes. They were spares to be installed by the Girl Guides in damaged sleepy-eyed dolls, which were the rage of that time.

There was no shortage of adult volunteers either. One unemployed man brought a small lathe and operated it there for us. The Crown Lumber Company brought scrap-ends of hardwood for mending coaster wagons. Roy Beavers, manager of the Club Cafe just up the block from the Toy Shop, kept us well supplied with simple meals and snacks, as did Jimmy Condon, who brought tasty treats from his Palace of Eats on the corner of Eighth and First Street West.

The Toy Shop "Santa's helpers" turned out doll houses, dolls, miniature cradles, rocking horses, and marble sets. Games such as checkers, Parcheesi, Snakes and Ladders, and Ludo were cannibalized and reassembled in complete sets. Even tricycles and doll carriages were put back on their wheels and repainted almost as good as new.

City-wide, the fire department joined the pre-Christmas activity by letting neighbourhoods know that fire halls should be used as drop-off points from which the toys would be forwarded to the shop.

In those pre–"batteries not included" days we youngsters, keen to be of help, tackled clockwork and springs, little flywheels, axles, and ratchets. I recall being very eager to please and be useful, a desire hampered only by the fact that I was all thumbs and still pretty sloppy with a paint or enamel brush.

One of my annual last-minute joys was playing assistant to Santa Claus. In his absence on a busy Christmas morning, I had the joyful task of handing out toys to the homeless children at the Salvation Army Booth Memorial Home, which was just a block from where we lived. The boxes of surprise gifts had been dropped off by my father, who made trips in his small truck from the Toy Shop to many points in town, as did a sizeable corps of fathers late on Christmas Eve.

When World War II thinned the ranks of Boy Scout leaders and other family breadwinners there was no lessening of the need for the Toy Shop's output. However, it had to fold by the end of the 1930s. Calgary's firemen, who had experienced the annual flood of reparable toys, took over the job from the Toy Shop and were worthy successors.

It is a pleasant thought that the idea which started with Leslie Sara's trip to see the post-Christmas bruised remnants of a department store's dismantled Toyland was successfully copied. Several cities on this continent and overseas found it to be a much-appreciated and heartfelt venture. It was a neighbourly scheme that was ripe for its time.

Opposite: *The world's first Toy Shop, organized in 1923 by Calgary Boy Scouts and Girl Guides with the support of the Herald Sunshine Society, operated for over a decade throughout the Depression. Each Christmas, refurbished toys and hampers were distributed to the city's needy families. The workers' parents, firemen, two local movie houses, and many firms helped the young Toy Shop volunteers ensure that no deserving children had a bleak Christmas.* **Courtesy Glenbow-Alberta Institute/NA–5368–15**

A Royal Command Performance

The decade of the 1950s, beginning with the celebration of the seventy-fifth year of its founding, was one in which Calgary received some notable additions to its make-up. A bumper crop of babies in the 1950s resulted in the city's head count breaking the 241,000 mark. An average of twelve babies per day drew their first breaths in the city during that decade, and thirty-one new citizens from other parts of Canada and countries abroad arrived in our midst daily, almost doubling our population before we reached the year 1960.

Visitors and traffic, in essence, added flavour to the ten-year span. In 1950 Viscount Alexander of Tunis, the governor general of Canada, and his family attended the Stampede. Princess Elizabeth and her husband, the Duke of Edinburgh, were here in October 1951. On the municipal level, that year Calgary played host to a national gathering of members of the Canadian Federation of Mayors and Municipalities.

In 1953, Canada's first native-born governor general, the Right Honourable Vincent Massey, came here. Her Royal Highness Princess Margaret stopped briefly in Calgary in July 1958 and, a year later, this time as queen, Elizabeth II and Prince Philip were back this way.

When the bunting was not out for Very Important Visitors, it fluttered before our eyes for Very Important Occasions that improved the pattern of much of Calgary's daily life. Traffic, as we fervently pursued our love affair with it, was in the forefront.

Midtown Calgary's most aggravating traffic bottleneck was Fourth Street West. Several mainline railway tracks as well as back-lane spur lines created the granddaddy of all level crossings. Striped wooden barrier arms equipped with red lights and bells, as well as trainmen on foot, waving red lanterns, kept streams of horse-drawn and motorized traffic at bay more than a score of times each day. There were mainline passenger and freight trains. There were merchandise-laden boxcars being shunted while distributing and collecting goods from dozens of midtown warehouses. Strings of grain cars were pushed and pulled back and forth as they serviced the Robin Hood Mills that spanned Fourth Street.

The T. Eaton Company wanted to build a department store on Eighth Avenue West between Third and Fourth, but not if the level crossing continued to annoy and delay the traffic flow. Twenty-four years after the opening of the store in 1929, the promised Fourth Street subway was completed despite absurd predictions that the towering mill buildings would topple into the excavation. The big dip under the multiple tracks caused rejoicing by wheeled Calgarians in 1953.

There was a great need to take some pressure off the traffic-laden Louise Bridge, so in 1953 work began on the Mewata Bridge over the Bow River at Fourteenth Street West. Hitherto, from the south, Fourteenth Street ended at the river, near the stables of the Strathcona Horse, behind the Armoury and the city incinerator on the west side of Fourteenth. The bridge was finished a year later.

Meanwhile, an elderly, narrow lattice-work span across the

Elbow was replaced by a wider concrete Elboya Bridge in order to handle the greatly increasing traffic flow on south Elbow Drive. While two bridges and a major subway eased the traffic flow in some locations, according to motorists another scheme presented a new hazard. In the midtown area some one-way avenues and streets were introduced and, for a while, much confusion reigned.

A traffic trendsetter in the retail core of the city was built by the Hudson's Bay Company in 1956. On the north side of Seventh Avenue, across from the store, some residences and the one-time Ranchmen's clubhouse were razed to make way for a multilevel automobile parking structure. The company created its own name for it—the Bay Parkade—and built an all-weather, glass-enclosed foot bridge above and across Seventh Avenue. An in-store illustrator, Norman Cowley, drew a huge coloured paper mural depicting two construction crews poised to "drive the last spike" or bolt or rivet. It showed the two bridge sections were not quite aligned, and Cowley's cartoon version of the hard-hatter's dismayed bewilderment was a joy to behold. It brought the store a lot of spectator business, and grins to some of the victims of the Seventh Avenue traffic vs. construction blues.

The weather on 18 October 1951 was bitterly cold but a miniature version of the Calgary Stampede was staged for Princess Elizabeth and the Duke of Edinburgh. The royal couple, helped down from a stagecoach by ranchers and stampede officials George Church and Jim Cross, stepped onto a symbolic Indian blanket leading to the grandstand from which they watched the rodeo. Courtesy Glenbow-Alberta Institute/NA–2785–21

Calgary's Temple
of Knowledge

*T*he Calgary Public Library, the first one in Alberta, opened its doors on Friday, 12 January 1912. Creation of "Calgary's temple of knowledge," as it was dubbed in our city's centennial year, was made possible, in large part, by the generosity of Scottish-born Andrew Carnegie.

The renowned United States steel manufacturer, having become very wealthy, chose as his philanthropic aim the distribution of grants for the construction of libraries throughout the continent. His initial gift to Calgary was one of $30,000 but, in order to complete the project, city council asked for, and was given, another $50,000. A 4.78-acre piece of land, obtained by the little city during a real estate boom in 1889, was chosen by plebiscite as a desirable central location for a public library.

Local sandstone was selected for the exterior by architects of Carnegie's choice, McLean and Wright, a firm based in Boston. Calgary stonemason George Christie was put in charge of construction, and local builder Richard A. Brocklebank was named McLean and Wright's on-site representative. The design was classical Greek but, for this structure, the heavy horizontal sandstone bases were meant to give the building the effect of having sprung from its surroundings. It was a concept well before the time of Frank Lloyd Wright, the champion of the ground-hugging style.

Surrounding the library building, Central Park took shape, under the supervision of H.G. Burrows, founder of the Calgary Horticultural Society. His park design called for stiff, formal, sweeping circular and ruler-straight paths, bowers of trees, two ornamental fountains, and geometrically precise flower beds. Impeccably kept by the city's parks department, this outdoor decor added to the atmosphere of solemnity we youngsters felt during our weekly excursions to "the Library," the only public one in town, to replenish our reading supplies.

Early in the planning of the formal layout, the park was foreseen as a popular leisure-time gathering place for Calgarians. A local building contractor, G.D. Thorpe, submitted a successful tender of $310 for the construction of a bandstand, a focal point at the west end of the park. Not long afterwards, having served its purpose briefly but well, the bandstand was demolished and replaced by a quite stately pavilion extending from north to south of the park, backing onto Fourth Street. Its centrepiece was a spacious white plaster band shell that, for many years, was used by various Calgary brass bands performing free outdoor public concerts.

It was commonly felt that there was a Grecian appearance to the elongated pavilion and bandstand. In truth, it had been patterned after its namesake, a similar structure in New York's Central

Opposite: *The Calgary Public Library opened on 12 January 1912 with a collection of five thousand books for a registered membership of 8,911, 16 percent of the city's population. Located in Central (now Memorial) Park, it was built of locally quarried Paskapoo sandstone. It is a special branch library now, but when a much larger library was erected in the centre of the city, for a short time the "old" library served as headquarters for the Glenbow archives.* Courtesy Glenbow-Alberta Institute/NA–4385–6

Park. Fortunately, for Calgarians, the land bound by Twelfth and Thirteenth avenues and by Second and Fourth streets West had been designated in perpetuity as parkland thanks to the foresight of Calgary-based, western Canadian federal land czar, William Pearce, an admitted nature lover and successful amateur horticulturist. I remember that for a long time Pearce's Red River cart spent its retirement years under the shallow overhang of the pavilion roof.

At the time the library opened, Calgary's population stood at only forty-four thousand, yet so impressive was the addition to Calgary's cultural life that the renowned and learned English poet, Rupert Brooke, gave it this praise after having visited Canada in 1913:

> As you traverse Canada from east to west they (public libraries) steadily improve. You begin in the city of Montreal which is unable to support one, and pass through the dingy rooms and inadequate intellectual provision of Toronto and Winnipeg. After that, the libraries and reading rooms, small for the smaller cities, are cleaner and better kept, show signs of care and intelligence; until at last, in Calgary, you find a very neat and carefully kept building stocked with an immense variety of periodicals, and an admirably chosen store of books ranging from the classics to the most utterly modern literature . . . Cross the Rockies and you're back among dirty walls, grubby furniture, and an inadequate literature again . . . but Calgary is hopeful . . . Few English towns could show anything as good.

Brooke was seeing the imprint of the early dedication of our first city librarian, Alexander Calhoun. Calhoun, a graduate of Queen's University and the University of Chicago, and his assistant William Castell both had served in Fort William (now the Lakehead). Alex Calhoun, his stiffly disciplined efforts backed by a splendid civic board, dedicated thirty-four years of his life as chief librarian.

He was a citizen of Calgary for sixty-eight years, during which time he was an originator of today's Canadian Library Association, a fervently active member of the CCF Party (predecessor to the NDP), first president of the Allied Arts Council, and recipient of a University of Calgary Honourary Doctor of Law degree. He died on 15 February 1979, just eight months before attaining his one hundredth birthday.

For a brief time our original "temple of knowledge," now known as the Memorial Park Branch, was able to make room for the first classes of the original Calgary University, which never did become a lasting reality.